641.5945 Tramonto, Rick.
TRAMONTO
          Fantastico!

DATE			

fantastico!

little
italian plates
— *from* —
rick tramonto's
kitchen

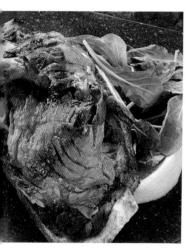

fantastico!

RICK TRAMONTO

with mary goodbody

PHOTOGRAPHS BY TIM TURNER

BROADWAY BOOKS | NEW YORK

PUBLISHED BY BROADWAY BOOKS

Published in the United States by Broadway Books,
an imprint of The Doubleday Broadway Publishing Group,
a division of Random House, Inc., New York.
www.broadwaybooks.com

BROADWAY BOOKS and its logo, a letter B bisected on the diagonal,
are trademarks of Random House, Inc.

Book design by Elizabeth Rendfleisch

Library of Congress Cataloging-in-Publication Data
Tramonto, Rick.
Fantastico! : little Italian plates from Rick Tramonto's kitchen /
by Rick Tramonto with Mary Goodbody. —1st ed.
p. cm.
Includes index.
1. Cookery, Italian. I. Goodbody, Mary. II. Title.

TX723.T735 2007
641.5945—dc22
2007001761

ISBN 978-0-7679-2381-1

PRINTED IN CHINA

1   3   5   7   9   10   8   6   4   2

First Edition

I would like to dedicate this book to my Lord and Savior Jesus Christ, who always leads me down the right road and who brings me through every storm every time. One verse in particular guides me through my life: "I can do all things through Jesus Christ which strengthens me." Philippians 4:13

To my wife and best friend, Eileen Tramonto, who helps keep me loved, humble, and close to God.

To my sons, Gio, Sean, and Brian, who keep me cooking and eating all the time. I love you guys.

And finally to my mom and dad, Frank and Gloria Tramonto, who have both gone home to be with the Lord. This book would not be possible without all of these great food memories with my crazy, loving Italian family. I love you and miss you.

contents

ACKNOWLEDGMENTS XI

introduction 2

CHAPTER 1
the glory of italian food 6

CHAPTER 2
assaggio | *a taste of something, a morsel* 10

CHAPTER 3
crudo | *raw, salted, and marinated* 40

CHAPTER 4
bocconcini | *small simple plates of quintessentially italian foods* 68

CHAPTER 5
bruschetta | *grilled bread with robust toppings* 110

CHAPTER 6
crostini | *little toasts with refined toppings* 132

CHAPTER 7
panini | *grilled sandwiches* 156

CHAPTER 8
cicchetti | *mini venetian-style sandwiches* 178

CHAPTER 9
antipasti | *little plates before the pasta* 190

CHAPTER 10
cheese | *the cheese course* 240

SOURCES *hard-to-find ingredients and equipment* 257
INDEX 263

ACKNOWLEDGMENTS

From Rick Tramonto:

Thanks to my friend and cowriter, Mary Goodbody, who for the third time has helped me put all of my thoughts and recipes into a book. I don't know how you do it, but I'm very grateful.

Thanks to my longtime friend and brilliant photographer, Tim Turner, who keeps me focused and challenges me to make every dish the best it can be during those long but fun photo shoots. Plate it again, plate it again, plate it again, plate it again . . .

Thanks to my supportive and loving family: Eileen Tramonto; Gio Tramonto; Sean and Brian Pschirrer; Paul and Dorothy Tramonto; Ed and Mary Carroll; Kathleen (Carroll), Lenny, Jesse, and Hannah Williams; and Joe and Bridget Carroll, who have shown me how to live and breathe outside the culinary world. Also thanks to the Tramonto family, the Lepore family, the Gentile family, the Sansone family, the Abbamonte family, the Faga family, and to any family that I forgot.

Thanks to my spiritual family, Pastors Gregory and Grace Dickow of Life Changers International Church, for their love, blessings, teachings, and prayers and for feeding me the Word of God. I can't thank you enough. Also to Van and Doni Crouch, Pastor Keith and Dana Cistrunk, Dr. Creflo and Taffi Dollar, Bishop T. D. Jakes, Jesse and Cathy Duplantis, Joel and Victoria Osteen, and Pastor James McDonald at Walk in the Word for their teachings and wisdom of the Word.

Thanks to my loyal agent and friend, Jane Dystal; my editor, Jennifer Josephy; and the great team at Broadway Books for their trust and faith in this book and in me.

A very special thanks to my chef and friend, Chris Pandel, as well as my sous chefs Tim Graham and Stuart Davis, for helping me test and organize these recipes. I couldn't have done it without them.

A special thanks to my partners at Cenitare Restaurants. And to my management team: Jeffrey Ward, Margaret McKinnon, and my assistant, Christina Fox.

I would like to also extend a warm thanks to my awesome staff at Osteria di Tramonto, Tramonto's Steak and Seafood, RT Lounge, Tru, and Osteria via Stato.

To my sommelier, Belinda Chang, or as I like to call her, Madam Chang the amazing wine girl, for her great wine notes in this book, her friendship, and her "fantastico" way of teaching us about wine with her version of "Wine Jeopardy." Thank you, Love.

I would also like to thank the town of Wheeling, Illinois, city of Chicago, Mayor Richard Daley and the food press for supporting me and allowing me to hone my craft in this great city.

Thanks to those who inspire me on a daily basis and who support my culinary efforts: Rich Melman, John Folse, John Besh, Chris Bianco, Pierre Gagnaire, Emeril Lagasse, Julia Child, Oprah Winfrey, Jose Andres, Ferran and Albert Adria, Jean-Georges Vongerichten, Alain Ducasse, Bobby Flay, Alfred Portale, Mario Batali, Patrick O'Connell, Nobu Matsuhisa, Martha Stewart, Guy Savoy, Juan Mari and Elena Arzak, David Bouley, Danny Wegman, Ina Pinkney (the breakfast queen), Randy Zweiban, Gray Kunz, Norman Van Aken, Martin Berasategui, Michael Lamonaco, Daniel Boulud, Michael Chiarello, Wolfgang Puck, François Payard, Greg Bromen, Jean-Louis Palladin, Alan Wong, Tom Colicchio, Roger Vergé, Eric Rupert, Frédy Girardet, Anton Mosimann, and Raymond Blanc.

Thanks to my supportive friends whom I rarely get to see because I work all the time. I love you guys. Thanks to Ron, Jill, Zeke, and Olivia Losoya; Jim and Linda Murdough; Ken and Marla Hines; Fenorris and Nicole Pearson; Peter Lepore; Larry and Julie Binstein; Vinnie and Theresa Rupert; Wendy Payton; Mike and Kelly Brosio; Jimmy Bonnesteel; Patti Street-Steeb; Jimmy, Ruby, and Ella Seidita; and my culinary partner in crime, Gale Gand.

A very special thanks to the vendors and the farmers across the country with whom I work every day. They work very hard to find and grow the best-of-the-best ingredients and products for me to use in my restaurants. This book would not be possible without them. Thank you and God bless you, big time.

From Mary Goodbody:

A heartfelt thanks to Rick Tramonto for including me in this project, from start to finish. I love this book! A big thanks to Jane Dystel, our agent, and Jennifer Josephy, our editor at Broadway, for their expert help and guidance. And thanks to Lisa Thornton for her help with the manuscript.

introduction

Italian food is my heritage. Italian food is what I love to cook. What's more, it's my soul. You see, I was raised in a large, noisy, loving Italian family where food was central to every activity, regardless of how ordinary or how celebratory. Meals could last for two or three hours, especially on Sundays, and no one found this surprising. For most Italians, this is the way it is, and it's the way we like it!

When you hear that I was an only child, you may wonder how I could call my family large. Easy. I was constantly surrounded by grandparents, aunts, uncles, and a gang of cousins. Sure, there were days when I was alone with my mother and father, but that changed in a heartbeat with the sound of footsteps on the front porch, the back door swinging open, or a car in the driveway. Let's face it. When you are part of an Italian family, whether in America or Italy, privacy is a relative term!

Rochester, New York, where we all lived, has a large Italian population. In those days, the neighborhoods were almost more Italian than similar areas in Rome or Naples. Shoe repair and barber shops were on every corner, hemmed in by music stores and Italian butchers and greengrocers. Old men dozed in the sun and children scampered from one backyard to the next. My dad—whom his friends called Chick, his family called Chickie, and everyone else called Frank—and I regularly drove the few miles between our house and Driving Park Avenue, where a row of three houses was home to most of my mother's family. My mother's parents, Adeline and Vincenzo Gentile, were quite elderly by then, as was Uncle Mario, who lived next door, and Dad determined that they needed regular visits. He bought them groceries from the Wegman's across the street and checked on the wine my grandfather made in the basement. When Vincenzo died, Adeline moved in with us for the last four years of her life.

My grandmas were longtime friends and once Adeline was part of our household, my father's mother, Liz DiPerno Tramonto, spent even more time with us. What a bonanza for a kid who loved being with his family and who loved to eat. Adeline had been born in Italy, and Liz's parents immigrated here from a small town near Naples. Both had grown up speaking Italian and both cooked as effortlessly as they breathed. What's the big deal? You cook, you eat, you love! They teased each other goodnaturedly about the superiority of their own cooking, and cheerfully ate each other's food, accompanied by red Italian wine.

And then there were the aunts. Or, to be more accurate, the great-aunts. Grandmother Tramonto was one of eight children, seven of whom were girls. These six aunts formed much of my culinary education, from Aunt Annie's escarole soup to Aunt Dot's veal parmesan and Aunt Theresa's sausage and peppers. On page 102, I have a recipe for Aunt Dorothy's tripe. I want to be perfectly clear that, in this case, Aunt Dorothy was not a Tramonto great-aunt but instead was married to my dad's brother, Uncle Paul. Most readers won't care about this distinction, but my cousins will!

My cousins and I were well-fed little rascals. My mom's brother Eddie had four kids—Kathy, Jean-Marie, Eddie junior, and Jimmie—and along with Peter and Phillip Lepore and Uncle Ray Tramonto's two daughters, Susie and Liz (whom we called Betty Ann to her dismay and our hilarity), I was one of those only children who consider their cousins more siblings than distant relatives.

As you read the short notes preceding the recipes in this book, my family's influence is apparent. We lived like most American-born kids in the sixties and seventies, playing baseball, watching TV, and going to school. But I bet we did so while eating better than most kings and captains of industry! No one was rich and everyone was blue-collar, but we had plenty to put on the table. My mother, aunts, and grandmothers shopped wisely and from people they knew and trusted. We tended large, overflowing vegetable gardens; we put up tomatoes and pickled peppers in the fall; we hung salumi in the basement; and we set aged Italian cheeses on plates for round-the-clock snacking. We often bought bread and freshly made pasta, but never hesitated to make our own.

I learned from all these skillful and confident home cooks. Not one of my aunts or grandmothers, much less my mother or father, would have dreamed that my children would grow up with classmates who didn't know how to cook. They would be appalled by the reality that preparing a nightly meal and expecting the family to sit down and eat—and eat extremely well—is now a rarity. I count my blessings that I grew up in the family I did and that I was taught to feel totally comfortable in the kitchen.

Sundays meant family. Family was part of every day, but there was something different about Sunday. It felt different, too. Most stores were closed, kids stayed close to home, and everyone went to church. After two hours of church, we stopped to visit elderly shut-ins and then gathered at one house, this big, rambling family of mine, for an afternoon of eating.

Everyone brought food, cooked, drank wine, and bounced the latest baby on available knees. Although I ended up leaving all this behind at age eighteen, traveled the world, and worked for and helped to open world-class restaurants in New York, London, and finally in my adopted city of Chicago, much of the food I cook today has direct roots to those Sunday feasts, and indeed to all the cooking that was so organic to my childhood and yet, I now realize, so special.

I left school early to help support my family, and although I never graduated from high school, my culinary education has been varied, intense, and neverending. By the time I was fifteen, I worked full time at Rochester's first Wendy's, often working alongside Dave Thomas himself. It was 1979 and Dave made regular visits to the few restaurants he then had, and to this day, I am grateful to him for creating an environment where a kid like me could thrive, move up, and acquire skills that would last a lifetime. I next found myself working at the Stathallen Hotel in Rochester, where under Chef Greg Broman's guidance, I discovered how much I love to cook. At Greg's urging, I moved to New York City to spread my culinary wings and found myself working for Alfred Portale at the Gotham Grill. Since, I have worked in and owned some of this country's top restaurants. I have worked in England with Raymond Blanc and Anton Mosimann and in France with Pierre Gagnaire and Michel Guerard. I have traveled as much as I could, absorbing, observing, and eating anything and everything as a way to broaden my informal but very determined culinary education—and relished every moment!

When I started traveling in Italy, I realized I was home. The food, the smells, the hospitality, and the warmth of the people I met and broke bread with propelled me back to my childhood in Rochester. My grandparents and their brothers and sisters, all born in Italy, had brought their homeland to the new world in palpable ways that resonated when I walked the streets of Naples or Milan, stopped at small *enotecas, osterias,* and *trattorias* in Venice and Florence, and drove through tiny, sun-splashed villages on the Amalfi Coast. But there was more. Italy is not a museum when it comes to its culinary genius. Its food is a living, evolving force, and I learn something new every time I set foot there.

My love of Italian food is as much contingent on the future as it is rooted in the past. I bring both perspectives to these small plates designed to offer bold, authentic flavors and new, exciting ones. I am fascinated by food history and how other generations cooked. Over the years, I have collected more than two thousand cookbooks and made sure I have every single issue of *Gourmet* and all the other food magazines to further augment my self-taught gastronomic education. I am intrigued by how much our culinary styles have changed—and yet stayed the same. Americans have always loved good cheese, summer tomatoes, simply cooked chicken, and perfectly ripened pears. We have been greedy to embrace the cooking of other lands, and then rushed to change it to make it our own. I find this inspiring and invigorating, and when I interpret Italian food for recipes such as those on the following pages and choose the wines to go with them, I look both backward and forward.

I may have been born to immigrants, I may have lived among people whose first language was Italian, but I was never encouraged to learn Italian myself. I pick it up as I travel in the country of my forefathers, but I am frequently stumped by it. I am never stumped by the food, however. I adore it and want to share my passion with you. But as everyone who travels or works with me knows, there are times when I am at a loss for the right word. And so, it's become a riotous inside joke among my staff: When I can't find the right Italian phrase, I smile broadly and exclaim, "*FANTASTICO!*"

I hope when you start cooking from this book, you will say it, too! Let the journey begin.

the glory
of
italian food

S mall bites, little plates—whatever you call them, these delicious tastes of assertive, mouthwatering foods are endlessly appealing. Whether you plan to serve an elegant first course, a meal made up of small dishes, or finger foods for a cocktail party, the recipes on these pages will blow your mind!

Okay, no lack of modesty there, but it's true. I have prepared these little dishes for years and never tire of them. For this book, I assembled a collection of recipes that celebrate all that is best about Italian food and Italian ingredients. I tailored them for the American home cook, who I hope will find them inspirational as well as accessible. Some are refined versions of the antipasti of my childhood, while others were motivated by frequent eating and drinking trips to Italy. (By the way: Is there any other kind of trip to Italy?)

I doubt I would get much argument when I say Italian food is universally loved. And why not? Think of fat-streaked cured hams, lightly pickled fish, and golden-green olive oil. Or how about pungent, earthy mushrooms; chubby, glistening olives, both green and black; syrupy balsamic vinegars; crumbly, salty cheeses; plump, juicy tomatoes; and crusty bread with a crumb so soft and pliant it mops up every last drop of goodness on a plate?

If you are salivating by now, read on. It gets better. As I put these and other ingredients together, the flavors conspire to explode in the mouth and make you hunger for more. The "more" may be another small, savory *assaggio* or *crudo*, a second glass of wine, or it may be the pasta course that comes next. Regardless, these treasures will prime your taste buds for all sorts of culinary adventures, regardless of their sophistication or simplicity.

Bruschetta, panini, bocconcini, and antipasti—heck, all categories of recipes in the book— can be made with nearly any ingredient that catches your fancy. Good news for the curious cook who eyes the jar of imported white anchovies or can of Italian tuna on the shelf and wonders what to do with it. Exhilarating for the intrepid shopper who is tempted by ruddy

Parma ham, crumbly truffle-specked Sottobosco cheese, or Black Mission figs. And equally thrilling for the cook who sees baby artichokes, cans of white ceci beans (also called chickpeas and garbanzos), wild mushrooms, fresh fava beans, and other more mundane foods in the markets and yearns to cook with them.

I have divided the book into nine recipe chapters. While it's tricky to categorize these little plates precisely, I explain the differences as I see them in the introductions to each chapter. But, if elsewhere you come across a recipe similar to one of mine that, say, is called a *cicchetti* rather than a crostini, no one is *wrong*. There is ample room for cross-pollination among these dishes.

Whether you indulge in a crostini, *cicchetti,* or a plate of fine Italian cheese, you will want a glass of wine to savor alongside it. These foods are nothing if not wine-friendly, and I am grateful to my friend and one of my sommeliers, Belinda Chang, for her spirited, thoughtful wine notes that accompany the recipes. Belinda shares my passion for all things Italian and my sense of fun when it comes to eating and drinking. I count on her to pour only the best wine for the food—and she succeeds every time!

go for excellence

The only hard-and-fast rule for these small taste treats is that the ingredients be the best you can find. This goes for meat and fish as well as for fruit, vegetables, and pantry items such as olive oil, vinegar, canned beans, canned tomatoes—even salt! Find a reputable butcher for prime or high-level choice beef and top-grade pork. Buy fish where turnover is constant and there is no odor in the air, except a whiff of the briny deep. Look for an Italian market or gourmet store that understands Italian salumi (all manner of cured meats), Italian sausage, and Italian cheese. Read through the recipes and their accompanying notes to learn more about these glorious gifts from the birthplace of the Renaissance.

Even if it means going a little out of your way, purchase fruits and vegetables in season and from local growers. I stand with the ever-increasing number of chefs who feel strongly about cooking with what is cultivated nearby, what is freshest, and what is least processed. How else, I ask you, can we guarantee the planet's abundance for our children and grandchildren?

This is the Italian way, too. When in Rome, literally do as the Romans do and feast on the produce from local farms and sip regional wines. Carry this philosophy to your own corner of the world. Of course, we hope you will buy the Italian wines Belinda and I suggest, but that should not be a problem. Experiment and have a good time with the food and the wine!

In the same spirit, buying seasonally can be fun. Where I live in Chicago, it's exciting to spot the first slender spring asparagus in the market, to know that the peach I buy in July will be so juicy my mouth will fill with pleasure, and that August's sun-ripened tomatoes will make all others taste like imposters! How about an azure October sky, red and gold leaves framing a country road, and a bushel basket of orchard-picked apples? Can you think of anything better? Because of this loyalty to the seasons, I arranged the recipes within each chapter so they progress from those best suited for springtime, through the summer and fall, to those perfect for a cold winter's night.

A number of the little plates in this book give the home cook license to experiment with ingredients that might be unfamiliar, such as razor clams or bresaola. You also can try some that might be too expensive to invest in more than now and then, such as truffles and foie gras. Here is a chance to indulge in a little luxury without making the ATM sputter with outrage! You need only a few drops of truffle oil or slices of prosciutto de Parma for the recipes. Pour a glass of mature Barolo and go for it!

When it comes to kitchen staples, I always think you should buy the best you can afford. For instance, I talk about olive oil on page 78 and salt on page 67. I believe that good-quality olive oil satiates more completely than any other fat, and because a drizzle is often all you need, why not pour the finest? The same goes for balsamic vinegar. When aged, it becomes sweet and syrupy. And expensive. Aged balsamic is one product where price nearly always indicates quality. When it comes to salts, as I explain later in the book, not all are created equal. I season mainly with kosher salt but play around with any number of the sea salts and specialty salts now on the market. They are fantastic for finishing a dish.

I feel just as strongly about fresh herbs, quality spices (definitely purge your cupboard of those old, dried-out, dusty little bottles), really good mustard, high-end butter, local honey, and freshly baked bread.

This holds true for the wine. Italians make world-class wines that drink splendidly with this food. Wine suggestions accompany every recipe in Chapters 2 through 8. For the antipasti and the cheese course, Chapters 9 and 10, look for an umbrella wine note at the start of each chapter; these foods are so versatile when it comes to wine, we figured a wine note could occupy a page or more!

Finally, don't neglect your equipment. No recipe in this book calls for anything that is not found in most well-stocked kitchens, but if you have not gotten around to replacing your mediocre knives with better ones or to buying that nonstick pan, do it now. It all matters. The knife will make slicing a tomato a breeze, and the pan will ensure success when you make a frittata. Cooking becomes more of a pleasure when you have a microplane grater for zesting citrus, a nest of nonreactive mixing bowls, and a few really good cutting boards. And your skill level improves, too. A little investment goes a long way.

After reading what I have written here, you get the idea. Go for excellence. Your guests will appreciate it, but most important, you will experience what I do when I serve the best and most honest food I can: the satisfaction of a job well done. Oh, and the chance to eat something that tastes *fantastico*!

CHAPTER 2

assaggio

a taste of something,
a morsel

I
decided to open the book with
these tiny bites because they are perfect
starts to just about any meal. Each one fills your
mouth with intense, powerful flavors and textures that set
your taste buds a-singing! Here are carefully chosen salty, sweet,
and sour flavors, where grilled shrimp cozy up to fat-streaked
pancetta, zucchini blossoms burst with smoky mozzarella cheese, and
fava beans dance in an orange-kissed bath. For me, these *assaggi* fall into
the same category as French *amuse-bouches*, those elegant little bites that
"amuse" or invigorate the palate before the meal begins.

ABOUT THE WINE

*Why limit yourself to one wine, when you could have a sip of something with each
taste? The assaggio course provides the perfect opportunity to open every bottle of
Italian wine that you have in your wine rack and in the fridge! Montepulciano
d'Abruzzo for the razor clams casino? Sure. Chianti for the roasted cipolline?
Absolutely! Fiano for the fava and yellow bean salad? Why not?
Remember, Italian wine is inherently designed to be enjoyed with
Italian food, and we have found that when you break the old
"white wine with fish, red wine with meat" rule,
you often discover a food and
wine nirvana!*

This salad speaks of spring, and when I first thought of pairing the beans with the radicchio, I knew it would taste splendid with the anise-flavored orange vinaigrette. My maternal grandmother, Adeline Gentile, made this vinaigrette more than any other, so star anise and Sambuca were staples in her kitchen. She spoke only Italian and had learned how to make the vinaigrette from her mother in Italy before emigrating to the United States. My grandmother's house was flanked by the houses owned by her two sisters; these three houses formed a little community where we always felt safe, welcome, and extremely well fed!

fava and yellow beans with radicchio, goat cheese, and anise-orange vinaigrette | *serves 4*

$1^1/_2$ cups shelled fava beans
$1^1/_2$ cups yellow wax beans
2 cups coarsely chopped radicchio
$^3/_4$ to 1 cup Anise-Orange Vinaigrette (page 13)
Kosher salt and freshly ground black pepper
1 cup crumbled goat cheese

1. Bring two pots of lightly salted water to a boil. Blanch the fava beans in one pot for 3 to 6 minutes or until tender. Drain and immediately submerge in ice-cold water. Drain again. Dry on paper towels.

2. In the second pot, blanch the wax beans for 2 to 3 minutes or until tender. Drain and immediately submerge in ice-cold water. Drain again. Dry on paper towels.

3. In a large bowl, toss together the radicchio, fava, and wax beans. Add the vinaigrette and season to taste with salt and pepper.

4. Divide the salad among 4 serving plates. Top each serving with goat cheese and serve immediately.

about the wine

You could, of course, pour a red wine to accompany this salad, but we don't want to go there. This spring salad needs an open bottle of white chilling in a bucket on the picnic table, within easy reach! The southern Italian white wine treat Fiano di Avellino can be found in modern styles where the fruit is highlighted over the nutty, piney flavors that tend to lead in more classic bottlings. MandraRossa in Sicily produces an outstanding example.

anise-orange vinaigrette | makes about 1^1/2 cups

1 shallot, chopped
Zest and juice of 1 orange
1 tablespoon honey
1^1/2 teaspoons sherry vinegar
1 teaspoon ground star anise
1 tablespoon Sambuca
1 cup extra virgin olive oil
Kosher salt and freshly ground black pepper
1 tablespoon chopped fresh basil

1. In a bowl, mix the shallot and orange zest. Add the orange juice, honey, vinegar, star anise, and Sambuca. Slowly whisk in the olive oil to emulsify. Season to taste with salt and pepper.
2. If using within 3 or 4 hours, stir in the basil and refrigerate. Otherwise, cover and refrigerate for up to 3 days. Stir the basil into the vinaigrette an hour or so before serving.

If you've never tried small, flat, disk-shaped cipolline onions, this is a good way to familiarize yourself with them. On a recent trip to Florence, when I ate at every little *enoteca* I could find, I discovered this dish, made extra special with aged balsamic vinegar and smoky, nutty chestnut honey. This honey is relatively easy to find in Italy, where chestnut trees grow, but is not as common here. If you must, use another mild honey.

roasted cipolline with aged balsamic and garlic bread crumbs | *serves 4*

16 cipolline onions
^{1}/4 cup olive oil
1 tablespoon minced garlic
1^1/2 teaspoons kosher salt
1^1/2 teaspoons freshly ground black pepper
^{1}/4 cup chestnut honey or other mild-flavored honey
Juice of 1 orange
3 cups chicken stock
2 sprigs fresh rosemary
2 sprigs fresh thyme
2 tablespoons Garlic Bread Crumbs (page 15)
2 tablespoons aged balsamic vinegar
1 teaspoon chopped fresh basil
1 teaspoon chopped fresh flat-leaf parsley

1. Preheat the oven to 350°F.
2. Bring a large saucepan of water to a boil and blanch the onions for about 1 minute. Drain and immediately transfer to a bowl of ice water to shock them. When cool enough to handle, drain again. Using a small sharp knife, trim the top and bottom of the onions and then peel the skins. They should slip right off. Leave the onions whole. (You can peel the onions without blanching, but blanching makes peeling far easier.)
3. In a large, deep skillet, heat 2 tablespoons of the olive oil over medium heat. When hot enough to coat the bottom of the pan, add the onions and garlic and cook for 4 to 6 minutes, or until lightly browned. Add the salt and pepper.
4. Reduce the heat to low, add the honey and orange juice, and stir to coat the onions. Cook for 5 to 7 minutes longer, or until the onions begin to caramelize.

5. Add the chicken stock, rosemary, and thyme and bring to a gentle simmer. Cook for 5 to 7 minutes, or until the stock is reduced by half and the onions are tender. Taste and adjust the amount of salt and pepper, if necessary. (The onions can be prepared in advance up to this point and refrigerated until ready to proceed. Bring the onions to room temperature.)

6. Transfer the contents of the pan to a baking dish just large enough to hold the onions in a single layer. Discard the herb sprigs. Sprinkle with the bread crumbs and bake for 4 to 6 minutes, or until the crumbs are lightly browned and the onions are warm.

7. Drizzle with the vinegar and remaining 2 tablespoons of olive oil. Garnish with basil and parsley and serve.

about the wine

Do the Florentine thing. These sweet onions will sing with the wines of the region. A bright, juicy Tuscan Chianti made from predominantly Sangiovese grapes, one that forgoes the new-fangled addition of fancy Cabernet, Merlot, or Syrah to the blend, is the right wine to pour.

garlic bread crumbs | makes about 4 cups

1 loaf day-old bread, such as ciabatta or baguette, cut into $1/4$-inch slices
$1/4$ cup olive oil
$1/2$ teaspoon kosher salt
$1/2$ teaspoon freshly ground black pepper
3 tablespoons unsalted butter
1 tablespoon minced garlic
$1/2$ cup freshly grated Parmigiano-Reggiano cheese

1. Preheat the oven to 350°F.

2. Lay the bread slices on a work surface and rub or brush both sides with half the olive oil. Sprinkle both sides with salt and pepper and lay the bread on a baking sheet.

3. Bake for 8 to 10 minutes, or until the bread is completely dry and golden brown. Check the bread every 4 minutes to make sure it does not overcook. Turn it once. Let it cool.

4. In the bowl of a food processor fitted with the metal blade, pulse the toasts until broken into $1/4$-inch pieces.

5. In a large sauté pan, heat the butter with the remaining 2 tablespoons of olive oil. When hot, add the garlic and cook for about 1 minute. Add the bread crumbs, tossing often until well coated. Spread the crumbs on a tray lined with paper towels to drain and cool.

6. When cool, transfer the crumbs to a bowl and toss with the Parmesan cheese. Use right away or store in an airtight container for up to 3 days.

Although I love anchovies, not everyone feels the same way about the tiny, salty fish. If you fall into this group, I suggest you try white anchovies imported from Italy. These are less sharp and cleaner tasting, and if you are like me, you will fall in love with them from first taste. My introduction to white anchovies was at an outdoor antipasti table near a bustling market in Venice, and I have kept a few cans on hand ever since. In this recipe, I decided to pair them with dandelion greens for my dad, Frank. While we had a big garden, our lawn was home to hundreds of dandelions and their greens, which my father picked all summer long and we made into salads. When Dad was dying a few years ago, he requested both anchovies and a dandelion greens salad; this is what I came up with for him.

marinated white anchovy and dandelion salad | *serves 4*

2 cups green beans
2 cups dandelion greens, stems trimmed
2 cups mizuna, stems trimmed
6 tablespoons Soft Herb Vinaigrette (page 18)
16 marinated white anchovy fillets, drained (see Note)
1 lemon, quartered
Pink Peruvian salt
Cracked black pepper

1. Bring a pot of salted water to a boil over medium-high heat.
2. Add the beans, let the water return to a boil, and cook for 2 to 3 minutes or until the beans turn bright green and are al dente. Drain, submerge in ice water, drain again, and set aside to cool.
3. In a large bowl, toss the dandelion greens and mizuna with the vinaigrette. Refrigerate for 10 minutes. During this time the greens will lose some of their bitterness.
4. Toss the blanched beans with the dressed greens just to coat lightly.
5. Divide the salad among 4 serving plates, piling it in the center of each plate. Arrange 4 anchovy fillets on and around each salad and serve. Garnish with a wedge of lemon, salt, and pepper.

(continued)

NOTE Use the best white anchovies you can find. I like Medusa brand anchovies, which are imported from Italy, packed in brine and oil, and sold in jars. They are available at some specialty shops and Web sites.

about the wine

Salted anchovies, peppery dandelion greens, and the herbs in the vinaigrette add up to a panoply of zingy flavors. A crisp, unoaked Sauvignon Blanc will wake up the palate and play nice with all of the green components in this dish. Italy's north would be the traditional place to find this style, but we have also found some good examples in the south from producers like Rivera in Puglia.

soft herb vinaigrette | makes about 1^1/4 cups

Juice of 1 lemon
1 tablespoon apple cider vinegar
1 teaspoon Dijon mustard
1 cup extra virgin olive oil
Kosher salt and freshly ground black pepper
1^1/2 teaspoons chopped fresh basil
1^1/2 teaspoons chopped fresh tarragon
1^1/2 teaspoons chopped fresh flat-leaf parsley

1. In a glass, ceramic, or other nonreactive bowl, whisk together the lemon juice, vinegar, and mustard. Slowly add the olive oil, whisking constantly until emulsified. Season to taste with salt and pepper.
2. If using within 3 or 4 hours, stir in the herbs and refrigerate. Otherwise, cover and refrigerate for up to 24 hours. Stir the herbs into the vinaigrette an hour or so before serving. If you leave the herbs in the vinaigrette for more than a few hours, they will brown.

I admit it: I think clams casino taste great, although some people laugh at me when I say so. When I was a kid, my mother made them every Christmas Eve, following the Italian tradition of serving only fish and seafood on that holy night, and I have continued the custom with my wife and sons. For me, clams casino are a way to connect to the family of my childhood. I put my own spin on them and use razor clams instead of the littlenecks Mom used. These are really, really good, and if you decide to make a lot of them for a party, I recommend the rock salt presentation at the end of the recipe. I add aromatic spices to the salt for interest and color, but if you prefer or time is an issue, you can simply present the clams on a bed of plain rock salt.

tramonto's razor clams casino | *serves 4*

RAZOR CLAMS
16 razor clams or 24 littleneck clams
$^1/_4$ cup olive oil
$^1/_2$ yellow onion, minced
$1^1/_2$ garlic cloves, crushed
1 cup white wine
Juice of 1 lemon
Kosher salt and freshly ground black pepper

CASINO FILLING
$^1/_2$ cup olive oil
1 cup diced bacon (about 10 slices)
1 cup diced celery
$^1/_4$ yellow onion, minced
1 garlic clove, minced
$1^1/_2$ teaspoons crushed red pepper flakes
2 cups panko (Japanese bread crumbs)
$^1/_2$ cup drained, chopped canned clams (see Note)
Juice of 1 lemon, plus 1 tablespoon grated lemon zest
$^1/_4$ cup Pernod
1 tablespoon chopped fresh chives
1 teaspoon chopped fresh tarragon
1 cup bottled or canned clam juice
$^1/_2$ cup freshly grated Parmigiano-Reggiano cheese
1 lemon, quartered

1. *To prepare the clams:* Gently scrub the clam shells with a soft brush. Transfer to a pot and cover with cold water. Set aside to soak for 1 hour. Change the water three times during the soaking to clean out any excess sand.

2. In a large saucepan, heat the olive oil over medium heat. When hot, sauté the onion and garlic for 3 to 4 minutes, or until the onion is translucent. Take care the garlic does not color.

3. Drain the clams and discard the soaking water. Add the clams to the pan and cook for 2 to 3 minutes. As they begin to open, add the white wine and lemon juice. Season to taste with salt and pepper. Cover tightly and steam for 5 to 6 minutes longer, until all the clams are fully open. Stir gently occasionally during cooking.

4. Lift the clams from the pan and when cool enough, gently pry open with fingers and scoop out the clam meat. (Discard any clams that do not open and the liquid.) Take care not to break the clam shells or their hinges. Razor clam shells are delicate. Clean the shells completely under cool running water and lay them flat on a baking sheet.

5. If necessary, rinse the clam meat under warm water to remove the sand sacks. Slice the clams into $^1/_4$-inch-thick pieces.

6. *To make the casino filling:* In a large sauté pan, heat the olive oil and cook the bacon over medium-high heat until slightly crisp. Lower the heat to medium and add the celery, onion, garlic, and red pepper and cook, stirring, for 5 to 6 minutes, or until the vegetables are softened.

7. Add the razor clams, panko, canned clams, lemon juice and zest, Pernod, chives, and tarragon and mix thoroughly. Slowly add enough clam juice to moisten the mixture; you will not need all of it. Simmer for about 5 minutes, or until heated through.

8. Let the mixture cool. To speed cooling, spread the mixture on a baking sheet.

9. Meanwhile, preheat the oven to 350°F.

10. Spoon the cooled filling into the clam shells, filling both shells of each clam, but do not pack it too tightly. Splash a little clam juice on each filled clam and sprinkle with Parmesan.

11. Lay the filled shells on a baking sheet and bake for 10 to 12 minutes, or until heated through.

12. Put 4 filled clams on each plate and drizzle them with the remaining clam juice. Garnish each plate with a lemon wedge.

(continued)

OPTIONAL ROCK SALT PRESENTATION
3 cups rock salt
$^2/_3$ cup whole star anise
$^2/_3$ cup pink peppercorns
$^2/_3$ cup black peppercorns
4 cinnamon sticks
Chopped flat-leaf parsley
1 lemon, quartered

In a large bowl, stir together the salt, star anise, and peppercorns. Spread equal amounts of the rock salt mixture on each plate. Make sure each plate includes a cinnamon stick. Arrange the clams on top of the salt. Garnish with parsley and a lemon wedge on the side of each plate.

NOTE If you want to use littleneck clams, you'll need 6 to 8 clams to yield the same amount of meat as the razor clams. Then follow the same procedure for cleaning and cooking the clams.

about the wine

Rich, smoky bacon and garlic take this seafood dish into red wine territory. We love this Tramonto holiday treat with an easy red like seaside Abruzzo's Montepulciano. Though often considered a mass-produced wine of variable quality, choose well and you will be rewarded. We have been impressed by producers like Masciarelli and La Valentina.

Many Italian home cooks, particularly those from my mother's generation, deep-fried zucchini blossoms without a thought—and their families benefited! Don't shy away from deep-frying at home. Use a heavy pot and, until you feel confident, a good deep-fat thermometer. Canola and high-oleic safflower and sunflower oil have higher smoking points than unrefined olive oil (although to confuse the matter, extra-light olive oil smokes at a higher temperature than these oils). My mom served zucchini blossoms in risottos and salads, and she also stuffed and deep-fried them. I like the stuffed, fried ones best and so developed this recipe, but however she served them was fine with me. They all reflected her name, Gloria, or Glo for short, and were glorious to me!

zucchini blossoms stuffed with smoked mozzarella and ricotta | *serves 4*

TOMATO RELISH

3 tablespoons olive oil

$^1/_4$ cup minced onion

1 garlic clove, minced

1 teaspoon crushed red pepper flakes

2 beefsteak tomatoes, peeled, seeded, and diced

Kosher salt and freshly ground black pepper

$^1/_4$ cup chopped fresh basil

ZUCCHINI BLOSSOMS

12 zucchini blossoms

$^3/_4$ cup grated smoked mozzarella cheese

$^3/_4$ cup fresh ricotta, drained

3 tablespoons freshly grated Parmigiano-Reggiano cheese

1 large egg yolk, plus 1 large egg

1 tablespoon chopped fresh flat-leaf parsley

Kosher salt and freshly ground black pepper

2 cups all-purpose or Wondra flour

2 cups canola oil, high-oleic safflower or sunflower oil, or extra-light olive oil

$^1/_4$ cup Basil Pesto (page 26)

4 crostini or other small toasts, for serving

1. *To prepare the relish:* In a sauté pan, heat 1 tablespoon of the olive oil over medium heat. When it's hot enough to coat the bottom of the pan, add the onion, garlic, and red pepper. Cook, stirring gently, for 4 to 5 minutes, or until the onions are translucent.

2. Add the tomatoes and cook, stirring, for 5 to 8 minutes, or until softened and most of the juices have evaporated. Season to taste with salt and black pepper.

3. Remove from the heat and stir in the remaining 2 tablespoons of oil and the basil. Cover to keep warm, and set aside.

4. *To prepare the zucchini blossoms:* Trim the blossom stems to about 1 inch.

5. In a small bowl, stir together the mozzarella, ricotta, 2 tablespoons of the Parmesan cheese, the egg yolk, and parsley. Season with salt and pepper.

6. Working with 1 blossom at a time, dredge the stem end lightly in the flour. Using great care, open the blossom. Fill it loosely with about $1\frac{1}{2}$ tablespoons of the cheese filling, pushing it toward the base of the blossom. Fold the ends of the blossom to completely enclose the cheese. Repeat with the remaining blossoms and set them on a plate. Discard the remaining flour.

7. In a small, shallow bowl, whisk together the whole egg and $\frac{1}{2}$ cup warm water to make an egg wash. Put the remaining cup of flour in another shallow bowl. Put the bowls next to each other on the work surface and set a baking sheet or platter next to them.

8. Dip each blossom in the egg wash, then let any excess drain off as you lift it out. Lightly coat in the flour and put on the baking sheet or platter. Repeat with the rest of the blossoms.

9. Pour oil into a large nonstick frying pan to a depth of about 1 inch or a little more. Heat over medium heat until hot. You will know the oil is hot enough when the air above it shimmers. Another test is to insert the clean end of a wooden spoon in the oil; bubbles will gather around it when the oil is hot. To be on the safe side, insert a deep-fat frying thermometer in the oil until it reaches 360°F.

10. Using a slotted spoon, gently submerge the blossoms in the oil. Fry for 3 minutes, turning once to brown evenly. Fry only 2 or 3 blossoms at a time and let the oil regain its heat between batches.

11. Lift the blossoms from the oil with the slotted spoon and drain on paper towels.

12. Season the blossoms with salt and pepper. (These are far better if served immediately, but if that's not possible, keep the blossoms warm in a 200°F oven.)

13. Put 2 tablespoons of the warm relish in the center of each of 4 serving plates. Put 3 blossoms around the relish. Dot the plate with pesto and garnish with a crostini.

about the wine

This dish celebrates warm days, and the wine that you drink with it should, too. An eccentric southern Italian wine from Basilicata is the one that we drink with this dish. Pipoli "Chiaro" Aglianco Bianco is a white wine made from a red wine grape that forgoes skin contact, but does not give up any flavor or texture.

basil pesto | makes about 2 cups

4 ounces pine nuts
8 ounces fresh basil leaves
$1^2/3$ cups extra virgin olive oil
$1^1/4$ cups freshly grated Parmigiano-Reggiano cheese
$1^1/2$ teaspoons finely minced garlic
$1^1/2$ teaspoons kosher salt

1. Spread the pine nuts in a single layer in a dry skillet. Toast over medium-high heat, stirring gently, for 2 to 3 minutes, or until golden brown and fragrant. Tip the nuts onto a baking sheet or platter and let cool.

2. Put the basil, olive oil, cheese, garlic, salt, and pine nuts in the bowl of a food processor fitted with the metal blade and process until smooth.

3. Transfer to a storage container with a tight-fitting lid, cover with about $1/2$ inch of oil so the pesto does not oxidize, cover, and refrigerate for up to 10 days.

Look for the biggest, greenest, freshest flat-leaf parsley leaves you can find, because the parsley stands in for other greens in this salad. Parsley grows easily, so every Italian I knew when I was growing up picked it from the backyard and tossed it as a salad. And those salads tasted great! Pair the parsley with tender young beets for indescribable small bites of freshness.

baby beets with flat-leaf parsley and mint vinaigrette | *serves 4*

3 cups plus 1 tablespoon kosher salt, plus more for seasoning
8 red baby beets, washed and trimmed but not peeled
8 yellow baby beets, washed and trimmed but not peeled
8 candy-striped baby beets, washed and trimmed but not peeled
4 tablespoons olive oil
1 teaspoon freshly ground black pepper, plus more for seasoning
2 cups fresh flat-leaf parsley leaves
Juice of 2 lemons
6 tablespoons Mint Vinaigrette (page 28)
$^1/_2$ cup shaved pecorino Romano cheese
Cracked black pepper

1. Preheat the oven to 350°F. Spread the 3 cups of salt over the bottom of a shallow roasting pan or sheet pan.
2. In a large bowl, combine the beets, 3 tablespoons olive oil, 1 tablespoon kosher salt, and 1 teaspoon pepper. Wrap the beets completely in large sheets of aluminum foil and transfer to the pan. The foil packets will sit directly on the salt. Roast for about 45 minutes, or until the beets are tender. Let the beets cool in the foil; this will make them easier to peel.
3. Peel each beet and cut in half, quarters, or slices. Transfer to a bowl.
4. In another bowl, toss the parsley with about a tablespoon of olive oil and the lemon juice. Toss and season to taste with salt and pepper.
5. Add the vinaigrette to the beets and toss until they are coated. Season to taste with salt and pepper.
6. Divide the beets among 4 serving plates, mounding them in the center of the plates. Arrange the parsley salad around and on top of the beets. Garnish each serving with cheese and cracked pepper and serve.

(continued)

The almost fruity, sweet beets with the crisp Mint Vinaigrette will be flattered by a white wine with high-density fruit tempered by a good dose of acidity. The Venica family in Friuli makes a Sauvignon Blanc from a famed single vineyard called "Ronco delle Mele" that screams orange and passion fruit and echoes the mint in the dish.

mint vinaigrette | makes about 1³/₄ cups

1 cup extra virgin olive oil
¹/₂ cup fresh orange juice
Zest of ¹/₂ orange
2 tablespoons fresh lemon juice
1 tablespoon minced shallot
1 tablespoon honey
Kosher salt and freshly ground black pepper
2 tablespoons chopped fresh mint

1. In a bowl, whisk together all the ingredients except the salt, pepper, and mint. Taste and season with salt and pepper.
2. If using within 3 or 4 hours, stir in the mint and refrigerate. Otherwise, cover and refrigerate for up to 3 days. Stir the mint into the vinaigrette an hour or so before serving.

My mantra throughout this book is to seek out the best. For these small plates you need only a little, so why not go for quality? Whether the olives you buy are from Italy, France, Spain, or California, buy ones you know have been carefully cured, packed, and stored. All olives, whether they are fresh green or ripe black olives, are cured when you buy them. I always take this a step further and mix the olives with olive oil, garlic, herbs, and perhaps a little citrus and red pepper flakes, as I do here. In the restaurant, we always have olives soaking in one mixture or another.

four-olive mix | *serves 4*

2 cups olive oil
3 garlic cloves, crushed
1 bay leaf
1 sprig fresh rosemary
$^1/_2$ lemon, sliced $^1/_4$ inch thick
$^1/_4$ cup finely grated orange zest
$1^1/_2$ teaspoons crushed red pepper flakes
$^1/_2$ cup Kalamata olives
$^1/_2$ cup Gaeta olives
$^1/_2$ cup Cerignola green olives
$^1/_2$ cup Ligurian olives

1. In a saucepan, heat the olive oil until warm over medium heat. Add the garlic, bay leaf, and rosemary. Take care the garlic does not brown. When the oil is very hot, remove from the heat.
2. Add the lemon slices, orange zest, and red pepper to the hot oil. Stir to mix, then add the olives and stir until well coated.
3. Let the olives cool in the oil. Transfer to a storage container with a tight-fitting lid and refrigerate for at least 24 hours and up to 3 weeks.
4. To serve, put the olives in a small bowl, along with the lemon slices, herbs, and garlic. Let come to room temperature.

about the wine

Don't stress about what to pour with this dish. Olives are one of those foods that seem to be made for enjoyment with wine and wine-based beverages. As we said before, anything in the wine rack will do. We just think that you should make it Italian!

I dedicate this recipe to my good friend and *paisan* Chef Chris Bianco, who owns Pizzeria Bianco in Phoenix, Arizona, which I could easily argue is the best pizzeria in the nation. Believe me, I am not alone! Chris is a soul mate who is as passionate about food and family as I am. When he taught me how to make this little dish, I fell in love with it. You can use any mushroom that is in season and you'll be very happy.

sautéed drunken wild mushrooms | *serves 4*

^{1}/2 cup olive oil

^{1}/2 cup diced onion

2 large garlic cloves, minced

1 cup quartered cremini mushrooms

1 cup quartered chanterelle mushrooms

1 cup sliced white mushrooms

1 cup diced portobello mushrooms

1 bay leaf

1^1/2 teaspoons chopped fresh thyme

1^1/2 cups dark beer

^{1}/4 cup balsamic vinegar

2 tablespoons unsalted butter

Kosher salt and freshly ground black pepper

1 tablespoon chopped fresh flat-leaf parsley

1. In a large sauté pan, heat the oil over medium heat until warm. Add the onion and garlic and sauté for 3 to 4 minutes, or until the onion is translucent. Add the mushrooms, bay leaf, and thyme and sauté for 5 to 7 minutes longer, until the mushrooms are just tender and still plump.
2. Add the beer and cook, scraping the pan, until reduced by half and a little syrupy.
3. Add the vinegar and stir to mix. Add the butter and stir the mushrooms as the butter melts. Season to taste with salt and pepper.
4. Divide the mushrooms among 4 serving plates, garnish with parsley, and serve.

about the wine

We poured a little red Cirò from Calabria for Chef Bianco, and he was sold. Made completely from the indigenous Gaglioppo grape, great examples will show ripe, dark fruit, tar, spice, and herbal notes. Librandi is one of our favorites, and we just think that you will have fun saying Gaglioppo three times fast to your friends!

Simply put, giardiniera is a mixture of pickled vegetables, and nobody made it better than my grandfather Vincenzo, who mixed up a big batch and put it up in glass jars every fall. It's a familiar site on antipasti plates and tastes good served alongside meats, grilled fish, and sandwiches. Cauliflower, carrots, and celery are nearly always included in the vegetable mix, but it's not unusual to find eggplant, cabbage, and peppers, too. This keeps for up to a month in the refrigerator, so you might want to make more than I suggest and enjoy it for several days. Or, follow Enzo's lead and can the giardiniera in glass jars so you can enjoy it for many months to come.

giardiniera | *serves 4*

MARINADE
1 cup Champagne vinegar
^{1}/2 cup sugar
^{1}/2 cup olive oil
1 teaspoon celery seed
1 teaspoon mustard seed
1 bay leaf

^{1}/2 cup olive oil
1 garlic clove, minced
1 teaspoon crushed red pepper flakes
1 teaspoon fennel seed
1 teaspoon dried oregano
1^1/2 cups chopped Napa cabbage
1 cup cauliflower florets
1 red bell pepper, cut into ^{1}/2-inch dice
1 cup diced carrots
2 cups diced celery
1 cup sliced onion
1 cup stemmed and quartered small white mushrooms
^{1}/2 eggplant, peeled and cut into ^{1}/2-inch dice
Kosher salt and freshly ground black pepper

1. *To make the marinade:* In a large saucepan, combine the vinegar, 1 cup water, sugar, olive oil, celery seed, mustard seed, and bay leaf. Bring to a boil over medium-high heat for 1 to 2 minutes, remove from the heat, and cover to keep hot.
2. In a large pot, heat the olive oil over medium heat. When hot, add the garlic, red pepper, fennel seed, and oregano and cook for 1 minute, stirring.
3. Add the vegetables and cook, stirring, for 8 to 10 minutes, or until the mushrooms release their moisture and begin to soften. Pour the hot marinade over the vegetables and stir well.
4. Remove the pot from the heat and allow to cool. Cover and refrigerate for 24 hours.
5. Taste and season with salt and black pepper. Serve or refrigerate for up to 7 days.

about the wine

The beauty of a great giardiniera recipe is that it lends itself to so many presentations and so many wine partners. When used to sop up bread, it's a great partner to Prosecco. When used in a dish with grilled fish, it can partner with one of Italy's illustrious white wines. Change the fish to meat, and the new dance partner becomes red wine. Experiment and play; there are no wrong answers.

Years ago, when I got my very first job as head chef at Chicago's Bella Luna restaurant, this was our most popular appetizer, a take on the old-school dish of scallops wrapped in bacon. I made it very Italian by using pancetta and still love these shrimp, impaled on toothpicks, on a plate of other finger foods. If you would like to serve scallops instead of shrimp, go for it! We make mayonnaise from scratch in the restaurant every day, but like you, I have not made it in my home kitchen in years. Why go to the effort when a good store-bought brand is just fine? Still, it's reassuring to make it every now and again, as I do here for the lemony aioli.

grilled shrimp wrapped in pancetta with lemon aioli | *serves 4*

^{1}/2 garlic clove, minced
1 large egg yolk, preferably from an organic egg
1 teaspoon Dijon mustard
1^1/2 cups extra virgin olive oil, plus more for brushing
Juice of ^{1}/2 lemon
Kosher salt and freshly ground black pepper
1 tablespoon chopped fresh basil
Vegetable oil spray
12 jumbo shrimp in the shell (10/15 count)
12 thin slices pancetta
1 tablespoon chopped fresh flat-leaf parsley

1. Put the garlic in a mixing bowl. Add the egg yolk and mustard and whisk. Still whisking, slowly add half of the olive oil to create an emulsion. When emulsified, pour in the rest of the oil, whisking well to combine. Whisk in the lemon juice and season to taste with salt and pepper. Stir in the basil. Set the aioli aside. (See Note.)
2. Prepare a charcoal or gas grill; the coals or heating elements should be medium hot. Lightly coat the grilling rack with vegetable oil spray to prevent sticking.
3. Peel the shrimp but leave the tails on. Devein and clean the shrimp.
4. Trim the pancetta slices so they are about 6 inches long. Wrap 1 shrimp in each slice of pancetta.
5. Brush the shrimp with olive oil and season with salt and pepper. Grill for 4 to 6 minutes, or until the pancetta is crispy and the shrimp is cooked through. Turn once.

6.   Arrange 3 shrimp on each plate and sprinkle with chopped parsley. Pass the aioli on the side for dipping.

NOTE You could substitute 1 cup of prepared mayonnaise and stir in the minced garlic, 2 tablespoons of extra virgin olive oil, the lemon juice, and basil. Season to taste with mustard, salt and pepper.

about the wine

This taste of shrimp kicked up with the flavors of crisped pancetta, mustard, and lemon can handle a richer, more voluptuous white wine for the accompanying sips. A Pinot Bianco with loads of fruit and a hint of citrus is a fun one to try, and our favorite comes from the master of the aromatic white wines Alois Lageder of the Alto Adige. We love the "Haberlehof" cuvée the best.

How can you beat these? The dates are warm, the cheese meltingly oozy, the walnuts crunchy . . . and when you pop one in your mouth, it explodes with sweet-and-salty goodness! These were served at every Tramonto family gathering when I was growing up in Rochester, New York, whether it was a big holiday like Christmas or Easter, or a family birthday. Thanks, Aunt Rose.

roasted medjool dates with gorgonzola, bacon, and toasted walnuts | *serves 4*

3 ounces Gorgonzola dolce (see Note)
1^1/2 ounces cream cheese
1^1/2 ounces slab bacon or 3 strips thick-cut bacon
12 Medjool dates
4 sprigs fresh rosemary
^{1}/2 cup finely chopped toasted walnuts
1 tablespoon extra virgin olive oil

1. Put the Gorgonzola and cream cheese in a bowl and set aside at room temperature to soften. When soft, mix the cheeses until well blended.
2. Preheat the oven to 350°F.
3. In a heavy-bottomed pan set over medium-low heat, slowly cook the bacon until the fat is rendered and the bacon is crispy. Drain the bacon on paper towels. When cool, cut into ^{1}/4-inch dice. Reserve 1 tablespoon of bacon fat and discard the rest.
4. Add the bacon to the cheese and mix gently. Stir the reserved bacon fat into the cheese mixture.
5. Make a slit in the top of each date and remove the pit. Gently open up the date, taking care to leave it attached at the base. Fill each date with about 1 teaspoon of the cheese mixture. As each one is filled, transfer it to a baking sheet. Scatter rosemary sprigs over the dates.
6. Bake for 2 to 4 minutes, just until the dates are heated through.
7. Arrange 3 dates on each of 4 serving plates. Sprinkle each one with chopped walnuts and a drizzle of olive oil. Garnish each with a rosemary sprig.

NOTE Gorgonzola dolce is a sweeter, milder Gorgonzola, aged for only a few months so that its flavor is not as pronounced as cheeses aged for longer periods. Look for it at a good cheese or gourmet shop.

about the wine

We can't resist going all the way with this treat in our hands. Sweet roasted dates with oozing blue cheese are wonderfully accompanied by an over-the-top red. Keep it all in Lombardy, the home of Gorgonzola and Bresaola, and try a red Sfursat di Valtellina like the "Fruttaio di Ca Rizzieri" from Rainoldi. Made from 100 percent Nebbiolo grapes, a portion of which go through a drying process similar to that used in Amarone, you are assured a sip of decadence to match each bite.

During one of my last trips to Milan, I got up at 4 A.M. and went to the fish market. By 6 A.M., I was sitting with the market guys, eating blood sausage and drinking wine. What a way to start the day! When I got back to Chicago I recalled the experience and paired blood sausage with crisp green apples and acetic saba vinegar. It's all about the memory of eating blood sausage with those guys in the Milan food market, savoring every bite, and laughing at their riotously bad jokes, told in broken English. Of course, as some of my staff like to point out, the fishermen got me to eat blood sausage at the crack of dawn—early even for me—so you could argue that the joke was on me!

grilled blood sausage with
green apples and saba | *serves 4*

Vegetable oil spray
4 links blood sausage (about 1 pound)
2 tablespoons olive oil
1 green apple, such as Granny Smith
2 cups watercress or pepper cress
1 tablespoon fresh lemon juice
1 tablespoon chopped fresh flat-leaf parsley
1 tablespoon torn fresh basil
Kosher salt and cracked black pepper
4 teaspoons saba vinegar (see Note)

1. Prepare a charcoal or gas grill; the coals or heating elements should be medium hot. Lightly spray the grilling rack with vegetable oil spray to prevent sticking.
2. Brush the sausages with olive oil and grill for 6 to 8 minutes, turning once or twice, or until heated through. Slice the sausages into 1-inch rounds and set aside.
3. Core the apple but do not peel it. Slice it very thin using a mandoline or a very sharp knife.
4. In a large bowl, combine the apple, cress, remaining olive oil, lemon juice, parsley, and basil. Toss to mix.
5. Add the sausages, toss, and season to taste with salt and pepper. Divide among 4 serving plates. Drizzle a teaspoon of saba over the mixture and serve.

NOTE Saba is concentrated grape juice, or must. You can buy it at some gourmet shops and online. You can make it yourself by letting very ripe white grapes ferment for 24 hours. The grapes should be so ripe that they easily release juice when pressed. Strain through a coffee filter or cheesecloth. Cook the juice over medium-low heat until it reduces to a syrup. Depending on how much grape juice you begin with, this can take several hours.

about the wine

There's no escaping the richness of blood sausage, but the saba and apple lighten the dish up a bit. An interesting partner to this is one of the wines made south of Milan in a region called Oltrepo Pavese. It is one of the few places where producers, such as Bruno Verdi, have success taming the difficult Pinot Noir grape, known there as Pinot Nero.

CHAPTER 3

crudo

raw, salted,
and marinated

This
group of recipes is far more
influenced by my travels in Italy and America
than by the food my mother and grandmothers served.
Crudo means "raw" or "uncooked" in Italy and refers to raw fish
and seafood. The idea of serving raw fish with an Italian flair has swept
the nation. Serving raw fish is not new to Italy, where fish just pulled from the
sea is sliced very thin and served with a drizzle of olive oil, a squeeze of lemon
juice, and some fresh herbs at small cafes up and down its long coastline. Italian-style
crudo differs from its Japanese cousin, sashimi, in the accompaniments. Both begin with the
freshest, best fish you can get your hands on. And it must be super fresh! For both, the fish
should be sliced very thin and with the grain. (Very cold, but not frozen, fish is easier to slice
than fish at room temperature.) Acidic fruits such as oranges, lemons, and pomegranates and
rich oils mingled with herbs, peppercorns, and thinly shaved fennel or onion make the sea bass,
tuna, or scallops on these small plates shine. When the plates are finished with a sprinkling of
exotic salt flakes, everything pops! I include a recipe for beef carpaccio, a classic Italian dish
composed of thinly sliced beef and a herbaceous, garlicky, lemony salsa verde. Not surprisingly,
these fragile, zesty dishes must be served as soon as they are prepared. But why wait? They
are that good!

ABOUT THE WINE
*A table laden with crudo is the ideal excuse to explore the aromatic whites of Italy. Racy
Pinot Grigio and Sauvignon Blanc or wildly perfumed Gewürztztraminer and Tocai
Friulano are called for here, and why not throw in a little Falanghina, Vernaccia, or
Erbaluce for good measure? Don't let the unusual grape varietal names
intimidate you. Most of the vino bianco of Italy provides us with the
fun possibility of experimentation without a major
financial investment.*

Hamachi is my favorite fish to eat raw—buttery, rich, and sexy. Similar to bluefin tuna, hamachi is a migratory fish sometimes called amberjack or buri; its golden flesh is favored by Japanese sushi chefs. This *crudo* is the result of one I ate in Barcelona, where the Spanish chefs are influenced by all other Mediterranean cooking. Let's face it, in Europe, as elsewhere, everyone borrows from everyone else. In Barcelona, I had a similar dish with a firm white fish, not hamachi, and to be honest, it was the grilled lemon that got me going. When I arrived home, I promptly looked for the best hamachi I could find and created this recipe. You can substitute sushi-grade tuna with equally good results.

hamachi carpaccio with piquillo peppers and grilled lemon | *serves 4*

1 lemon, plus juice of $^1/_2$ lemon
$^1/_2$ cup olive oil
Grated zest of 1 orange
$^1/_2$ cup finely diced plum tomatoes
$^1/_2$ cup finely diced piquillo peppers or pimientos (see Note)
2 tablespoons julienned fresh basil
1 tablespoon chopped fresh chives
1 tablespoon chopped fresh mint
Fleur de sel (see page 67)
Cracked black pepper
1 pound sushi-grade hamachi or yellowtail

1. Set a cast-iron skillet over medium-high heat until very hot (or heat a countertop grill).
2. Cut the lemon into $^1/_2$-inch slices. Pour the olive oil into a shallow bowl and dip the lemon slices in it to coat both sides. Cook the lemon slices in the hot skillet for about 30 seconds, or until lightly charred on both sides. Remove and set aside.
3. In a nonreactive bowl, mix the lemon juice, orange zest, tomatoes, peppers, basil, chives, and mint. Season to taste with salt and pepper.
4. Slice the hamachi $^1/_2$ inch thick and arrange on 4 plates. Spoon the tomato-pepper mixture over the hamachi and let it sit for 5 minutes before serving. Season to taste lightly with salt and pepper and garnish each plate with charred lemon slices. *(continued)*

42 fantastico!

NOTE Piquillo peppers are imported from Spain, where they are grown, wood-roasted, and then packed in jars. They are increasingly available in our supermarkets and specialty stores, although I suggest you read the label carefully to make sure they are the real deal. Jarred pimientos are an adequate substitute, but are not nearly as good in this recipe as piquillos.

about the wine

Smoky piquillo peppers, orange, mint, and tomato all in one dish poses quite a challenge when choosing a wine. With the richness of the fish, a white with some weight is called for, and we choose a Tocai Friulano from Friuli. Our friends from New York, the Bastianich family, make a superb example at their winery in the region formally known as Friuli-Venezia Giulia.

I had never seen a home cook cure fish until I visited a family friend's home in Rome and was served a sublime cured salmon. This was before I opened Tru in 1999, and until then, I had only known chefs to cure foods in restaurant kitchens. But this Roman home cook took curing salmon in stride and served it with a lovely fennel salad dressed with killer olive oil—I was sold. You do not have to cure the full amount of Cured Salmon for this recipe but there's no reason not to if you love it as much as I do. Use it for snacks, hors d'oeuvres, and to dress up bagels or eggs. If you prefer, cure only a pound and adjust the amount accordingly. Either way, once cured, it keeps for a week, if refrigerated. You will be pleased beyond your wildest dreams and you, too, will say "*fantastico!*"

cured salmon with shaved fennel
and radish salad | *serves 4*

$1^1/2$ cups thinly sliced red radishes (about a dozen radishes)
$1^1/2$ cups julienned raw fennel (1 large bulb), fronds reserved
$1/2$ cup torn fresh basil
$1/3$ cup Lemon Vinaigrette (page 47)
Kosher salt and freshly ground black pepper
12 very thin slices Cured Salmon (page 46)

1. In a small bowl, toss the radishes, fennel, and basil with 3 or 4 tablespoons of the vinaigrette. Taste and correct the seasoning with salt and pepper if needed.
2. Lay the salmon on a large platter so that the slices overlap slightly. Scatter the salad over the salmon. Drizzle with as much of the remaining vinaigrette as desired. Season again with pepper, garnish with reserved fennel fronds, and serve.

about the wine

Chef Tramonto had this dish in Rome, and chances are good that they drank a wine from the Lazio with it. Superstar wine consultant Riccardo Cotarella owns a lion's share of the vineyards in the "Est! Est!! Est!!!" region of the Lazio, and his Trebbiano-based wine is a glass of crisp, racy goodness perfect for enjoying with the cured salmon.   *(continued)*

cured salmon | makes one 2^1/2-pound salmon

2^1/2 pounds medium-thick salmon fillets

2 tablespoons coarsely chopped fresh thyme

2 tablespoons coarsely chopped fresh tarragon

2 cups kosher salt

1 cup sugar

2 tablespoons crushed fennel seed

2 tablespoons grated orange zest

1 tablespoon grated lemon zest

1 tablespoon crushed juniper berries

1 tablespoon crushed star anise

1 tablespoon cracked black pepper

1. Remove any skin, bones, and bloodlines from the salmon.
2. Put the thyme and tarragon in a bowl and add the salt, sugar, fennel seed, orange and lemon zest, juniper berries, star anise, and pepper. Mix well.
3. Spread about half the salt mixture in the bottom of a shallow, flat pan large enough to hold the salmon in one layer. Lay the salmon on top and then spread the rest of the salt over the fillets. Cover tightly with plastic wrap and refrigerate for at least 24 hours and up to 28 hours.
4. Lift the salmon from the pan and scrape off the salt crust. Rinse the salmon well under cold running water and then pat dry with paper towels. Wrap again in plastic and refrigerate for 3 to 4 hours longer. This sets the cure.
5. With a sharp slicing knife, slice the fish on the bias into thin slices and proceed with the preceding recipe. You can also serve the cured salmon on its own. Wrap the cured salmon tightly in plastic wrap and put in a rigid plastic container. Refrigerate for up to 7 days.

lemon vinaigrette | makes about 1 cup

1 cup extra virgin olive oil
Juice of 2 lemons
Kosher salt and freshly ground black pepper
1 tablespoon chopped fresh basil
$1^1/2$ teaspoons chopped fresh tarragon
$1^1/2$ teaspoons chopped fresh cilantro
$1^1/2$ teaspoons chopped fresh chives

1. In a small bowl, whisk together the olive oil and lemon juice. Season to taste with salt and pepper.
2. If using within 3 or 4 hours, stir in the herbs and refrigerate. Otherwise, do not add the herbs but cover the vinaigrette and refrigerate for up to 24 hours. Stir the herbs into the vinaigrette an hour or so before serving. If you leave the herbs in the vinaigrette for more than a few hours, they will brown.

Unlike the other recipes in this chapter, this one is not so much inspired by my travels in Italy as by the beef carpaccio my grandmothers and aunts prepared for special family celebrations, primarily those that fell in the spring and summer. Although I add an apple and pea shoot salad to dress up the plate, the carpaccio of my childhood was garnished with nothing more than salsa verde, which is a wonderfully versatile sauce to have on hand, and which holds very well if you cover it with good olive oil. Because I am a trained chef with good knife skills, I cut the carpaccio far thinner than my grandmother did. If you have these skills or an electric slicer, slice it thin. However, the beef does not have to be superthin, so use a sharp knife and do your best. Partially freezing the beef makes it easy to slice. You can also pound it thin between plastic wrap. And please, buy the best beef you can afford. Prime beef from a butcher you know and trust is the best course.

beef carpaccio with green apple and pea shoot salad and salsa verde | *serves 4*

1 pound rib eye or fillet of beef
Kosher salt and cracked black pepper
1 tart green apple, such as Granny Smith
1 cup pea shoots or watercress leaves
$^1/_2$ cup thinly sliced celery, plus $^1/_4$ cup chopped celery leaves
$^1/_2$ cup extra virgin olive oil
Juice of 1 lemon
1 tablespoon chopped fresh basil
1 tablespoon chopped fresh chives
$^1/_4$ cup Salsa Verde (page 50)

1. Put the beef in the freezer for 1 to 3 hours, until partially frozen.
2. Slice the beef paper-thin and arrange it in a slightly overlapping layer on each of 4 plates or a single large platter. Season with salt and pepper.
3. Cut the unpeeled apple in half or quarters and remove the core. Slice very thinly.
4. In a mixing bowl, combine the pea shoots, celery, celery leaves, and apple. Add the olive oil and lemon juice and toss. Add the basil and chives, toss, and season with salt and pepper.
5. Mound the salad in the center of the overlapping slices of beef. Drizzle Salsa Verde around the outside of the plate, season again with salt and pepper, and serve. *(continued)*

It may seem strange to pour a white wine with beef, but with all of the green, citrus, and bright notes in this dish, it is the right thing to do. We have learned that the wine choice is almost always about the sauce, not the protein. Try a Sicilian Alcamo, a blend of aromatic white wine grapes such as Inzolia, Catarratto, and Grecanico. Cusumano makes a great example.

salsa verde | makes about ³/4 cup

¹/2 cup olive oil
1 teaspoon finely minced garlic
¹/4 cup chopped fresh flat-leaf parsley
1 tablespoon drained, chopped capers
1 tablespoon chopped fresh oregano
1 tablespoon chopped fresh basil
¹/2 teaspoon crushed red pepper flakes
1 shallot, finely minced
Juice of ¹/2 lemon
Kosher salt and cracked black pepper

1. In a small saucepan, heat the oil over medium-low heat until barely warm. Add the garlic and cook for about 1 minute, until warmed through. Do not let the oil boil or the garlic turn color.
2. Remove from heat and add the parsley, capers, oregano, basil, red pepper, shallot, and lemon juice. Stir gently and season to taste with salt and black pepper.
3. Set aside to cool, then transfer to a glass or plastic container, cover, and let cool to room temperature.
4. If you are not ready to use the salsa right away, cover and refrigerate for up to 1 day. Let it return to room temperature before serving.

I had lunch at Beccofino restaurant in Florence and was impressed that the waiters shaved bottarga at the table over a trio of fish tartares. It reminded me of shaving truffles or perhaps cheese, and of course the sun-dried fish roe perfectly accented the raw fish. I don't always have bottarga on hand, so I list it as an optional ingredient. If you can find some, though, please try it. And don't neglect the salt.

tartare of halibut, pickled red onion, and shaved bottarga | *serves 4*

1 pound halibut, skinned, boned, and bloodline removed
^{1}/4 cup diced yellow bell pepper
Juice of 1 lime
Grated zest of ^{1}/2 lemon
1 tablespoon chopped fresh cilantro
1 tablespoon chopped fresh chives
1 tablespoon freshly grated ginger
1^1/2 teaspoons finely chopped Calabrian chile pepper or other hot chile, optional
^{1}/2 cup extra virgin olive oil, plus more for drizzling
Kosher salt and freshly ground black pepper
1 cup Pickled Red Onion and Cucumber (page 52)
^{1}/4 cup shaved bottarga, optional (see Note)
Sea salt or Sicilian Sea Salt (see page 67)
Coarsely ground black pepper
4 lemon wedges

1. Chop the halibut fine and transfer to a stainless steel mixing bowl. Set the bowl inside a larger one filled with ice and water. Cover and refrigerate both bowls for at least 30 minutes.
2. In a mixing bowl, mix together the bell pepper, lime juice, lemon zest, cilantro, chives, ginger, and chile pepper, if using. Whisk in the olive oil and set aside if not using right away. Whisk before using.
3. Remove the chilled fish from the refrigerator and start adding the dressing, a little at a time and tasting as you go, until flavorful and moist, but not drenched. Season to taste with salt and black pepper.

(continued)

4. Mound equal amounts of the halibut tartare on each of 4 small plates. Arrange the pickled vegetables next to the tartare and garnish each plate with shavings of bottarga, if desired, a sprinkling of sea salt and coarse pepper, and a lemon wedge. Drizzle with olive oil and serve.

NOTE Bottarga is salted, pressed, and dried mullet or tuna roe, which is shaved or grated and used to flavor a number of Italian dishes as well as those from Sardinia and Sicily. Once the roe is salted, it is pressed between weights and then dried in the sunshine for a few months. Mullet bottarga, called *mugine*, is preferred to the tuna, called *tonno*, although both are tasty and either works well here. You may have to buy bottarga off the Internet or from a specialty store.

about the wine

Poderi del Paradiso in Tuscany blends Vernaccia and Chardonnay together in their "Biscondola" cuvée to tasty effect. The Chardonnay fleshes out the sometimes simple and light Vernaccia, and helps it to stand up to the concentrated sea flavors of the bottarga. Italy offers many blended whites with a bit more texture and density that will work here, but stay away from the barrel-aged wines for these dishes.

pickled red onion and cucumber | serves 4

2 star anise
1 bay leaf
1^1/2 teaspoons black peppercorns
1^1/2 teaspoons coriander seed
1^1/2 teaspoons fennel seed
2 cups rice wine vinegar
2 cups Simple Syrup (page 53)
1^1/2 cups thinly sliced red onions (1 to 1^1/2 onions)
1^1/2 cups thinly sliced cucumber (1 cucumber)
Kosher salt and cracked black pepper

1. Lay a double thickness of cheesecloth on the countertop and pile the star anise, bay leaf, peppercorns, and coriander and fennel seeds in the center. Gather the sides of the cheesecloth and tie the opposite corners together (or tie with kitchen twine) to make a bundle, or sachet.
2. In a saucepan, combine the vinegar and syrup. Add the sachet and bring to a boil over medium-high heat. As soon as the mixture boils, remove it from the heat and let cool to room temperature. Discard the sachet.

3. Meanwhile, in a small bowl, combine the onions and cucumber. Season to taste with salt and pepper and set aside.
4. Pour the cooled liquid over the onions and cucumber. Cover and refrigerate for at least 8 hours but no longer than 2 days. Serve at room temperature.

simple syrup | makes about 2 cups

2 cups sugar

1. In a medium saucepan over medium heat, combine the sugar and 2 cups water and stir until the sugar dissolves. Raise the heat and bring to a boil; then remove from the heat and set aside to cool.
2. Transfer to a container with a tight-fitting lid and refrigerate for up to 1 week.

Because I love oysters, I can't write a book without including them. I owe a large part of my keen appreciation of oysters to my good friend Chef John Folse. John champions his home state's food, and about two months before Hurricane Katrina in 2005, he took me to all his favorite oyster haunts in and around New Orleans. Two weeks after the hurricane, I traveled back to Louisiana to help John and his team cook for the relief workers, the Coast Guard, the guys from FEMA, and the army. It was mind-blowing to spend time in St. Bernard Parish. We also traveled to Mississippi and cooked for the homeless at a church. It was a very humbling experience and my prayers and ongoing support go out to the people of those hard-hit areas and especially to my friends in New Orleans, a city that is dear to my heart for its overall spirit and remarkable food culture. I'll be back soon for more oysters!

oysters with red wine vinaigrette | *serves 4*

16 seasonal oysters, such as Bluepoint, Belon, or Malpeque (see Note)
About 16 cups crushed ice
1 cup high-quality aged red wine vinegar
Juice and grated zest of $^1/_2$ lemon
$^1/_4$ cup extra virgin olive oil
$^1/_2$ cup finely diced plum tomatoes
3 tablespoons thinly sliced scallions, green parts only
3 tablespoons minced shallots
2 tablespoons julienned fresh basil
Kosher salt and freshly ground black pepper
4 lemon wedges

1. Using a vegetable brush, scrub the oysters under cold running water to remove any debris. Spread some of the ice over a tray, place the oysters on top, and refrigerate for at least 1 hour, until very well chilled.

2. Take the tray from the refrigerator and leave the oysters in place. Spread a second tray with fresh ice and set aside. Wrap one oyster at a time, in a heavy kitchen towel or similar cloth, holding it so that the hinged side is exposed and the rest of the shell is encased. Bunch the cloth around the exposed end of the oyster to protect the hand holding it through the cloth. Insert an oyster knife into the apex of the hinge and then push, twist, and lift to loosen the top shell. Run the knife along the top of the shell, severing the muscle that holds the meat in

place. Discard the top shell and take care to keep as much of the oyster liquor in the bottom shell as possible. As each shell is opened, lay the bottom shell holding the oyster and the liquor on the tray spread with fresh ice. Refrigerate the tray with the oysters.

3.   In a mixing bowl, stir together the vinegar, lemon juice, and lemon zest. Whisk in the oil, then stir in the tomatoes, scallions, shallots, and basil. Season to taste with salt and pepper.

4.   Spread more crushed ice on a serving platter and transfer the oysters to it, nestling them into the ice to keep them icy cold. Top each oyster with about a tablespoon of vinaigrette, garnish the platter with a lemon wedge, and serve.

NOTE   The oysters I use in this recipe are Atlantic or Eastern oysters and are defined by their elongated, uneven, bumpy shells. Most of the oysters sold in the United States fall into this general category. Other types of Atlantic oysters include Chesapeake, Wellfleet, and Kent Island oysters.

about the wine

Okay, so we said do white wine with *crudo*, but the vinaigrette for this dish is made with red wine vinegar. Vinegar with red wine is a tough sell for the palate, so we'll compromise, and recommend a rosé. Cabanon in Lombardy makes a textured rosé from the Bonarda grape that makes a nice fruity companion to the oysters.

Marinated swordfish is common in Venice, where I first tried it at a restaurant called Al Diauola Osteria, one of a string of *enotecas* where the fishermen and fishmongers congregate to eat and drink wine after their morning labor. These holes-in-the-wall are nothing fancy, everyone stinks of fish, and everyone eats fish while sharing fish stories, each one more unbelievable than the next. But guess what? Most are true!

marinated swordfish with mint and preserved meyer lemon | *serves 4*

1 pound center-cut swordfish, bloodline removed
1 cup diced plum tomatoes
1 cup shaved plain artichoke hearts
Juice of $^1/_2$ lemon
2 teaspoons grated Preserved Meyer Lemon zest (page 79) or ordinary lemon zest
$^1/_2$ cup extra virgin olive oil
1 tablespoon chopped fresh mint
1 tablespoon chopped fresh chives
1 teaspoon pink peppercorns, crushed
$^1/_2$ teaspoon ground star anise
Kosher salt or Hawaiian Volcanic salt (see page 67)
Freshly ground black pepper

1. Slice the swordfish paper-thin or as thin as possible and arrange the slices on a platter so they overlap slightly.
2. In a small bowl, mix the tomatoes, artichoke, lemon juice and zest, olive oil, mint, chives, pink peppercorns, and star anise. Season to taste with salt and black pepper.
3. Pour the marinade over the swordfish. Refrigerate for 10 to 15 minutes and serve. (Do not leave the fish for longer or the acid in the marinade will start to "cook" the fish.)

about the wine

Simple, fresh Gavi made in Piedmont from the Cortese grape makes a nice background for the artichoke, preserved lemon, and spices that pop in this dish. Wines from producers like La Scolca and Contratto are in order here. (Remember: stay away from the fancy oak-aged ones; they tend to be more expensive and less *crudo*-friendly.)

preserved meyer lemon | makes 6 preserved lemons

6 Meyer or other lemons
1 cup kosher salt
1 cup sugar
1 tablespoon coriander seed, crushed
1 tablespoon fennel seed, crushed
1 tablespoon crushed star anise
1 tablespoon coarsely ground black pepper
Pinch of saffron

1. Poke holes in the lemons with a fork.
2. In a mixing bowl, combine the salt, sugar, coriander and fennel seeds, star anise, pepper, and saffron. Add the lemons and toss to coat.
3. Transfer the lemons and salt-herb mixture to a clean glass jar with a tight-fitting lid. Set aside in a cool dark place or in the refrigerator for 4 weeks. Shake the jar occasionally.
4. Lift the lemons from the jar and rinse with cool running water. Pat dry. If not using right away, transfer the lemons to a clean jar, cover, and refrigerate for up to 6 months.

I remember a raw fish dish with Moscato grapes and lime salt that I was served at the Conterno Winery during Vin Italy Fair, the Italian wine expo. The winemaker invited me to his home in Giacomo for lunch, and while he used turbot, I decided to try this with fluke. It was a totally refreshing crudo. *Fantastico!*

fluke with cucumber, lime salt, and moscato grapes | *serves 4*

1 pound fluke, halibut, or similar white fish, boned, and bloodline removed, if necessary
1 cup Moscato or other green seedless grapes, halved
^{1}/2 cup extra virgin olive oil
1 seedless cucumber, diced
Juice of 2 limes
1 tablespoon chopped fresh cilantro
1 tablespoon chopped fresh basil
1 tablespoon diagonally sliced scallion, green parts only
1 teaspoon crushed red pepper flakes
Lime Salt (page 59)
Cracked black pepper

1. Slice the fluke paper-thin or as thin as possible and lay the slices on a platter so they overlap slightly.
2. In a bowl, mix together the grapes, olive oil, cucumber, lime juice, cilantro, basil, scallion, and red pepper. Season to taste with Lime Salt and black pepper.
3. Spoon the marinade over the fluke and set aside at room temperature for about 10 minutes. (Do not leave the fish for longer or the acid in the marinade will start to "cook" the fish.)
4. Season with a little more Lime Salt and serve.

about the wine

You may be tempted to serve this dish with a Moscato from Piedmont, but beware, nearly all of those wines are sweet. We find instead that a floral, zippy Erbaluce from Piedmont is the better white to serve here. Luigi Ferrando and Orsolani make many different wines with the Erbaluce grape, and while still, dry styles work best with the fluke, we love them all.

lime salt | serves 4; makes about $^1/_2$ cup

$^1/_4$ cup coarsely grated lime zest
$^1/_4$ cup Maldon salt (see page 67)

In a spice or coffee grinder, grind the lime zest and salt until the oils are released from the lime and the salt is slightly lime colored. Keep, covered, for up to 2 days.

VARIATIONS

To make orange or lemon salt, substitute orange or lemon zest for the lime zest.

I remember spending a few days with my wife, Eileen, in Portofino in Italy, which is simply beautiful. One day, we went to a big seaside restaurant called Il Delfino, arriving about eleven in the morning and staying through the early afternoon. We sat on the terrace, with the water glinting blue and silver and the fishing boats bobbing on the horizon, and ordered raw tuna with pomegranates, lemon, and basil. That memory inspired me to create this dish. It's a great way to serve one of my all-time favorites, raw ahi tuna, but be sure to buy the freshest, best fish you can. Look for bright color, firm flesh, and no odor except a faint whiff of the sea.

crusted ahi tuna with
pomegranate vinaigrette | *serves 4*

TUNA
$^1/_2$ cup crushed coriander seed
$^1/_2$ cup fennel seed
$^1/_3$ cup black peppercorns
$^1/_3$ cup pink peppercorns, optional
Two 8-ounce log-shaped pieces sushi-grade ahi or bluefin tuna
Kosher salt

VINAIGRETTE
1 cup fresh or store-bought pomegranate juice
$^1/_3$ cup high-quality sherry vinegar
Juice of 1 lime
1 medium shallot, minced
1 teaspoon Dijon mustard
1 cup extra virgin olive oil
1 tablespoon chopped fresh basil
1 tablespoon chopped fresh chives
Sea salt, Cyprus Black salt, or Black Cyprus sea salt flakes (see page 67)
Cracked black pepper
Pomegranate seeds, optional
4 lime wedges

One of the best lunches I've had in recent years was at Cantinetta Antinori in Florence during a recent trip to Italy, so when I came home, I set about recreating it. When I travel, I keep copious notes about the food I eat, and for this, I jotted down that the blood oranges and green olives "were magic" together.

sea bass carpaccio with blood orange, capers, and green olives | *serves 4*

1 red onion, thinly sliced
1 cup red wine vinegar
1 tablespoon sugar
Kosher salt and cracked black pepper
$^1/_2$ cup extra virgin olive oil
Juice of 1 lemon
$^1/_2$ cup chopped Cerignola or other large green olives
$^1/_4$ cup drained small capers
1 tablespoon chopped fresh basil
1 tablespoon chopped fresh cilantro
$^1/_2$ teaspoon crushed red pepper flakes
2 blood oranges, peeled and segmented
1 pound sea bass fillets, skinned and boned
Sea salt, Peruvian Pink salt, or Australian Murray River salt (see page 67)

1. In a bowl, combine the onion with the vinegar and sugar and stir gently to mix. Season to taste with salt and black pepper and refrigerate for about 1 hour.
2. In another bowl, whisk together the olive oil, lemon juice, olives, capers, basil, cilantro, and red pepper. Add the chilled onion slices and the orange segments, toss gently, and season to taste with salt and black pepper.
3. Cut the sea bass into thin slices and arrange them on a serving platter. Spoon the vinaigrette over the fish, garnish with a little cracked pepper and sea salt, and serve.

about the wine

The key to choosing wine for most of these *crudo* dishes is *keep the oak away* to avoid off, astringent, or overly tannic tastes. Opt for styles that are clean, fresh, and unmolested by oak barrels.

salt

Like most chefs, I season with kosher salt rather than standard table salt. It is pure, with no additives, and has no metallic aftertaste. Plus, because its crystals are a little larger than fine table salt, you can feel it in your hand and see where it falls on the food. This makes it less likely you will oversalt. On these pages, the food I present is full of flavor and many of the ingredients are intrinsically salty, so careful seasoning is important. I suggest you, too, reach for the kosher salt.

On the other hand, I am intrigued by the specialty salts that are available today. These are rarely used to season food as it cooks, but instead to finish a dish. Play with these salts and you'll be surprised, as I was, by how different they taste from each other and how just a little sprinkle can bring a dish to attention! I use Hawaiian Red, Pink Peruvian, Australian Murray River, and Cyprus Black salt, as well as the more familiar Maldon salt and, of course, lovely, flaky French fleur de sel. But look around: There are many, many different salts, ranging in color from pure white to red and inky black and harvested in every corner of the world. To learn more and to order some exotic salts, go to www.salttraders.com or www.saltworks.us.

salt glossary

AUSTRALIAN MURRAY RIVER SALT: Apricot-colored, flaky salt from the Murray River's underground brine deposits. It has a mild flavor and the flakes melt easily into hot food.

CYPRUS BLACK SALT: This salt is made from Mediterranean flake salt mixed with activated charcoal. The color is great and the flavor distinct and mild.

FLEUR DE SEL: From France's Brittany coast, this salt is ivory colored and imparts the pure flavor of the sea.

HAWAIIAN RED SALT: This salt is enriched and colored by the naturally occurring red clay of the islands, which adds iron. The salt has great flavor and color.

KOSHER SALT: Made from granular salt that is pressed into flakes. No additives.

MALDON SALT: A natural sea salt made by the Maldon Company in Great Britain. Many find it tastes of the sea and has a distinctive, pleasing saltiness, so less is needed.

PINK PERUVIAN MOUNTAIN SALT: Mined in the Andes Mountains in naturally fed salt ponds, this salt is pale pink with a pleasant but strong flavor.

CHAPTER 4

bocconcini

small simple plates
of quintessentially
italian foods

Bocconcini
are delicious little morsels, just
several small mouthfuls of amazing Italian
foods put together to achieve sensory perfection. Eat
only one and you are ready for the next course of a
conventional meal. Assemble sets of two or three, pour some great
Italian wine, and you have a light meal. Many Americans think of small
balls of fresh mozzarella cheese when they hear the term *bocconcini*, and while
many chefs and cheese purveyors *mean* the cheese when they list bocconcini, this
is not what I mean in this chapter. Instead, I have put together plates of traditional
flavors, textures, and aromas that will transport you to the white-washed walls of a
small trattoria in Italy as only the real thing can. I also make these plates a little larger
than those for the *assaggi*, which makes them a little more versatile.

ABOUT THE WINE

*Many would argue that the quintessential Italian wine is that red stuff that comes clad in a
wicker basket. Well, we certainly agree that Sangiovese (from Chianti and other regions)
rules the roost. Topping the list at approximately 11 percent of vines planted, Sangiovese
is the most-planted grape in Italy, and takes many names, many flavors, and many
partners. Prugnolo Gentile, Brunello, Morellino, and Sangioveto are just a few of
the names that it goes by in Tuscany alone. Don't limit yourself to the
Sangiovese of Chianti and Tuscany, though. You'll find excellent
examples in Umbria, Emilia-Romagna, the Marche, and oh
yes, even in Napa and Sonoma!*

Artichokes are eaten throughout Italy, where you find them in just about everything from pastas and risottos to salads. Not surprisingly, they are familiar on little plates, too. I particularly like to cook with baby artichokes, which are so tender you do not have to worry about tough outer leaves or prickly chokes, as you do with larger artichokes. I also use them for centerpieces. What looks more beautiful than a bowl piled with baby artichokes?

baby artichokes with lemon-garlic bread crumbs | *serves 4*

$^1/_2$ cup olive oil

1 onion, diced

4 garlic cloves, minced

1 teaspoon crushed red pepper flakes

20 whole baby artichokes, cleaned and halved (see Note)

1 cup white wine

1 quart chicken stock

2 sprigs fresh thyme

1 bay leaf

2 tablespoons unsalted butter

Juice of 1 lemon

Kosher salt and freshly ground black pepper

2 cups Lemon-Garlic Bread Crumbs (page 71)

1 tablespoon chopped fresh flat-leaf parsley

2 tablespoons freshly grated Parmigiano-Reggiano cheese

1. In a heavy-bottomed pot, heat the olive oil over medium heat. Sauté the onion, garlic, and red pepper for 3 to 4 minutes or until translucent.
2. Add the artichokes and sauté for about 10 minutes or until they start to soften.
3. Add the wine, raise the heat so that the wine simmers briskly, and cook, stirring the pan with a wooden spoon to scrape the bottom, until the wine reduces by half.
4. Add the stock, thyme, and bay leaf and simmer for 30 to 40 minutes, until the artichokes are completely tender. Whisk in the butter and lemon juice and season to taste with salt and black pepper.
5. While the artichokes finish cooking, preheat the oven to 350°F.

6. Lift the artichokes from the liquid with a slotted spoon and transfer to a baking dish just large enough to hold them in a single layer. Spoon enough of the liquid over the artichokes to moisten them generously and cover the bottom of the dish.

7. Generously sprinkle the crumbs over the artichokes and bake for 10 to 12 minutes, until the crumbs are golden brown.

8. Garnish with parsley and Parmigiano-Reggiano and serve.

NOTE To clean baby artichokes, trim the stems so that they are flush with the base of the leaves and remove one or two layers of the outer leaves. The number of leaves you remove will depend on the size of the artichoke. If there are any spiny tops, snip them off with a pair of scissors. Baby artichokes can be as small as walnuts or as large as cue balls, and depending on their size, some will need more attention than others. Larger ones will have tougher outer leaves, for instance. Because they are so small and tender, there is no need to worry about a fuzzy center called the choke; it's perfectly edible in these little vegetables. Baby artichokes are not actually immature globe artichokes, but are simply small specimens.

about the wine

We dare you to drink red wine with artichokes. Keep the tannin level in the wine low, the fruit component high, and victory will be yours! We have shown this dish with a fruity style of Rosso di Montalcino, another incarnation of the Sangiovese grape, to first angry, then surprised, and then rave reviews. Many serious Brunello di Montalcino producers make the less ponderous Rosso; we like Il Poggione and Carpaz's wines with this dish.

lemon-garlic bread crumbs | makes about 4 cups

^{1}/2 teaspoon kosher salt
^{1}/2 teaspoon freshly ground black pepper
1 loaf day-old bread, such as ciabatta or baguette
^{1}/4 cup olive oil
3 tablespoons unsalted butter
1 tablespoon minced garlic
^{1}/2 cup freshly grated Parmigiano-Reggiano cheese
^{1}/4 cup grated lemon zest

1. Preheat the oven to 350°F.

2. In a small bowl, combine the salt and pepper.

(continued)

3. Cut the bread into $^1/_4$-inch slices and lay on a baking sheet. Rub 2 tablespoons of the olive oil into both sides of the bread. Sprinkle both sides with the salt and pepper mix.

4. Toast the bread in the oven for 10 to 12 minutes, or until completely dry and golden brown. Check it every 4 or 5 minutes to make sure it does not brown too much.

5. Transfer the toast to the bowl of a food processor fitted with the metal blade and pulse just until the crumbs are about $^1/_4$ inch thick. Do not process until fine.

6. In a large sauté pan, heat the butter and the remaining 2 tablespoons of oil over medium-high heat. Add the garlic and cook for about 45 seconds. Add the crumbs and toss often until coated.

7. Spread the crumbs on a large paper-towel–lined tray or platter. When cool, toss the crumbs with the cheese and lemon zest. Use immediately or store in an airtight container for up to 2 days.

NOTE Instead of toasted day-old bread, you can substitute panko (Japanese bread crumbs). Sauté them in the oil, butter, and garlic and proceed with the recipe.

I never saw broccoli in my grandmother's kitchen, but she always had broccoli rabe on hand. We called the tender, leafy vegetable "rabi" or "rapini" and ate it happily in many guises. Most often, it was cooked quickly in olive oil and garlic, as I do here. You can serve this warm or at room temperature, as a small plate or alongside cheeses and salumi.

broccoli rabe with slivered garlic | *serves 4*

1 pound broccoli rabe
^{1}/3 cup olive oil
1 tablespoon sliced garlic
1 teaspoon crushed red pepper flakes
1 tablespoon unsalted butter
Juice of 1 lemon
Kosher salt and cracked black pepper
Shaved Parmigiano-Reggiano cheese
2 tablespoons chopped fresh basil
1 tablespoon chopped fresh flat-leaf parsley
1 tablespoon chopped fresh chives

1. Bring a saucepan of lightly salted water to a boil and blanch the broccoli rabe for 5 to 8 minutes, until bright green and almost tender. Drain and immediately submerge in ice-cold water. Drain again.
2. In a sauté pan, heat the olive oil over medium heat. Sauté the garlic and red pepper just until the garlic turns light brown. Add the broccoli rabe and butter and heat through. Add the lemon juice and season to taste with salt and cracked black pepper.
3. Divide the broccoli rabe among 4 serving plates. Garnish with the cheese, basil, parsley, and chives, and serve.

about the wine

Emilia-Romagna is the home of Parmigiano-Reggiano, aceto balsamico (balsamic vinegar), and some tasty Sangiovese. Because the soils tend to be more fertile in these vineyards north of their Tuscan brethren (and as we know, vines that suffer produce wines that are more intense and full of character), these Sangiovese-based wines tend to be softer and simpler. Umberto Cesari is one of the most famous wineries in the region, and his Sangiovese di Romagna is a nice, easy quaff to accompany this dish.

This dish has been part of my repertoire for years—I introduced it at Trio, where I was the chef in the early 1990s. When I was growing up, we usually ate fennel shaved thin and served with lemon and pepper. Now I like it braised, too, and find that raw or cooked, with its mild licorice flavor, fennel has a natural affinity for oranges. For this little plate, I pair it with plenty of orange juice and finish the dish with grated orange zest. I always use a microplane grater to remove the zest from citrus fruit and highly recommend you invest in one of these marvelous kitchen tools.

braised fennel with orange | *serves 4*

4 fennel bulbs, plus 1 tablespoon finely chopped fronds
8 tablespoons (1 stick) unsalted butter
$^1/4$ cup diced onion
3 oranges
1 tablespoon Pernod
$1^1/2$ cups chicken stock
Kosher salt and freshly ground black pepper

1. Preheat the oven to 350°F.
2. Cut the fennel bulbs into quarters. Remove and discard the root ends.
3. In an ovenproof braising pan, heat 4 tablespoons of the butter over medium heat. Add the fennel and onion and cook for about 2 minutes, or until the onion is softened.
4. Grate the zest from 1 orange and reserve. Cut all 3 of the oranges in half and squeeze the juice into the pan. Add the Pernod, ignite it to burn off the alcohol, then bring the liquid to a brisk simmer, scraping the bottom of the pan with a wooden spoon to deglaze. Simmer until the liquid reduces by half, then add the chicken stock. Season to taste with salt and pepper.
5. Stir in the remaining 4 tablespoons of butter. When incorporated, cover the pan and bake for about 20 minutes, or until the fennel is tender.
6. Transfer to a serving bowl. Season to taste with salt and pepper. Garnish with the reserved orange zest and fennel fronds and serve.

about the wine

Vernaccia di San Gimignano from Tuscany is a mouthful to say, and it can also be a mouth-filling white wine. Often blended with Chardonnay and/or Vermentino (like the famous "Terre di Tufi"), those wines made from the Vernaccia grape on its own offer lifting acidity, floral bouquet, and a nice foil for the licorice-y fennel and Pernod.

This little dish demonstrates how Italians are eating now: fewer big meals and more small plates with exquisite combinations of flawless foods. Grilled radicchio is great as a summertime bocconcini when your grill is ready and waiting for the next great thing. Try to find radicchio rosso di Treviso, which, unlike the more familiar rounded variety of radicchio, is elongated. Look for tight heads with fleshy red leaves, as these will fare best on the grill. But don't neglect this dish if you can find only the round heads of radicchio. Any grilled radicchio is fantastic.

grilled radicchio di treviso with
garlic vinaigrette | *serves 4*

VINAIGRETTE

$1/2$ cup extra virgin olive oil

$1/3$ cup freshly grated Parmigiano-Reggiano cheese

$1/4$ cup sherry vinegar

2 garlic cloves, minced

1 tablespoon grated lemon zest

1 tablespoon chopped fresh flat-leaf parsley

1 teaspoon fresh lemon juice

RADICCHIO

2 heads radicchio rosso di Treviso

$1/4$ cup olive oil

Kosher salt and freshly ground black pepper

1 tablespoon freshly grated Parmigiano-Reggiano cheese

1. *To make the vinaigrette:* Put the olive oil, cheese, vinegar, garlic, lemon zest, parsley, and lemon juice in a blender and blend until emulsified. Cover and chill for at least 4 hours and up to 6 hours. Let the vinaigrette come to room temperature before whisking and serving.

2. *To make the radicchio:* Prepare a gas or charcoal grill. The heating element or coals should be medium-hot.

3. Cut the radicchio heads lengthwise into quarters. Don't trim the root ends. Lay the quarters on a baking sheet, coat with olive oil, and season with salt and pepper. Do your best to keep the radicchio quarters neat and intact. *(continued)*

4. Lift the radicchio from the pan and lay on the grill. Grill for 3 to 4 minutes on each side, or just until wilted. Do not let the ends char.
5. Transfer the radicchio to a cutting board and when cool enough, cut into $^1/_3$-inch strips. Discard the root ends. Transfer the radicchio to a mixing bowl.
6. Toss the radicchio with 4 to 6 tablespoons of the vinaigrette and the cheese. Season to taste with salt and pepper and divide among 4 serving plates.

about the wine

Radicchio can have a strong, bitter bite, but the caramelization on the grill mellows the intensity of the bitterness. We like this smoky dish with a young Chianti Classico that has a high Sangiovese content (producers are allowed by law to add as much as 25 percent other grapes to the blend). Producers like Collelungo and Ricasoli make styles that are appropriate with this dish.

olive oil

Olive oil is one of my favorite cooking ingredients and is intrinsic to my cooking. I can't emphasize how important it is to use great olive oil. Italy, France, Spain, and Greece all produce terrific olive oil and you will want to sample various oils from these countries. Tasting it is like tasting wine—it has almost as much to do with aroma, texture, and color as with taste. Depending on the strength and intensity of the oil, some are better for finishing a dish while others are better for marinating, cooking, or flavoring food. I use extra virgin olive oil for uncooked preparations, such as vinaigrettes, and rely on pure olive oil for cooking. I recommend Terre Bormane olive oils, which are Italian oils available at health food stores, gourmet shops, and some supermarkets. Opalino and Albis are the two Terre Bormane oils I use most often for marinating, finishing, and even cooking. I have developed my own line of Tramonto signature olive oils. My friend Lucio Gomiero, who owns the Vignalta Winery in Veneto, Italy, is making them for me. As a sideline to this task, Lucio is also one of the largest radicchio farmers in the world.

Whatever oil you choose, don't hold back when you use it.

I had eaten *fonduta* many times, but never appreciated it until I traveled with my good friend Chef Paul Bartolotta through Tuscany and the Piedmont region of Italy. Paul is from Chicago and now has a restaurant in the Wynn Hotel in Las Vegas called Bartolotta's. With his knowledgeable guidance and enthusiasm spurring me on, I finally tasted the real deal and discovered what I had been missing. Fontina cheese has been produced in Italy's Val d'Aosta since the Middle Ages, and perhaps longer. (For more on Fontina, see pages 120 and 253.)

fonduta | *serves 4*

^{3}/4 pound young Fontina cheese without rind, such as Fontina Val d'Aosta
1 cup heavy cream
2 tablespoons unsalted butter
4 large egg yolks
1 tablespoon white truffle oil
Kosher salt and freshly ground black pepper
Black or white truffles (as many as you can afford), shaved, optional
12 slices Rick's Basic Crostini (page 134)

1. Cut the fontina into thin slices and lay in a shallow bowl. Add the cream and refrigerate for at least 4 hours and up to 6 hours.
2. Reserving the cream, lift the cheese slices from the cream and set them in the top of a double boiler, fondue pot, or other saucepan.
3. Add the butter and 3 tablespoons of the cream. Set over simmering water (do not let it boil) and stir just until the cheese melts and can be pulled into strings.
4. In a mixing bowl, whisk the egg yolks with the remaining cream. Add to the cheese mixture, still over simmering water, and stir until thick and smooth. Stir in the truffle oil and season to taste with salt and pepper.
5. Divide the *fonduta* between 4 small bowls and garnish with shaved truffle, if desired. Serve with the crostini.

about the wine

This is a chance to raid your wine stash and drink one of those bottles that you have been saving for a special event. Drink something magnificent, such as a perfectly aged bottle of something with a name ending in *-aia*. Sassicaia, Ornellaia, and Tassinaia are all names of Super Tuscan wines that when spoken aloud, make our mouths water!

Salumi refers to all dry-cured Italian-style meats and sausages. Great chefs such as Tom Colicchio, Lidia Bastianich, Mario Batali, and Paul Bertolli are introducing them to a new generation of Americans, who may not realize what an incredible variety is available. Thanks to these chefs for bringing this artisan tradition back to the culinary fore. What an inspiration! One summer when I traveled in Italy, I was served salumi with peaches just about everywhere I went and although it was a combination I had never before tried, it made perfect and delicious sense and stayed with me after I returned to Chicago.

salumi with peaches and watercress | *serves 4*

8 thin slices Finochionna salumi
12 thin slices Tuscan salumi
12 thin slices Sulmitti pepperoni
2 ripe peaches or nectarines
$1/2$ cup olive oil, plus more for drizzling
Juice of 1 orange
Juice of 1 lemon
2 bunches watercress
1 tablespoon chopped fresh mint
1 tablespoon chopped fresh basil
Kosher salt and cracked black pepper
1 ounce pecorino cheese, shaved

1. On a serving platter, arrange the salumi and pepperoni slices in an overlapping pattern.
2. Without peeling the peaches, remove the pits, slice the fruit into thin wedges, and put in a bowl. Add the olive oil, orange and lemon juice, watercress, mint, and basil and toss gently. Season to taste with salt and pepper and toss again.
3. Spoon the salad next to the salumi. Drizzle both the salumi and salad with olive oil, garnish with the cheese, and serve.

about the wine

One of the grapes used in Marsala production, Inzolia (also known as Insolia, also known as Ansonica), like Viognier, can produce a highly perfumed, voluminous-textured white reminiscent of stone fruits and flowers. Count Marzotto's estate Baglio di Pianetto produces two tasty examples: "Ficilgno," which blends Viognier and Inzolia, and the 100 percent Viognier "Piana del Ginolfo."

Like most of you, I can't get enough of summer's tomato crop, and one of the most exciting things to have happened to this harvest in recent years is the revival of heirloom tomatoes. Grown from seeds passed down through the generations, the fruits have not been crossbred or otherwise manipulated. The result? Magnificent tasting, juicy tomatoes that pair beautifully with the rich, creamy burrata cheese and syrupy aged balsamic. Burrata is the creamy remnants of mozzarella, enclosed in a bag of pulled curd. The creamy cheese is hard to find outside of Italy but if you run across it, try it. If you can't find it, substitute high-quality fresh mozzarella.

There are many heirloom varieties. Some of my favorites are Brandywine, Black Krim, Cherokee Purple, Amish Paste, Green Zebra, Purple Calabash, Yellow Ruffled, Pineapple, and Old-Fashioned Red. You will note that not one of these is called beefsteak or Big Boy. Heirlooms may be large or small, oddly shaped, or pear shaped. What they all share is good flavor. When you see unfamiliar tomatoes at a farmer's market this summer, try a few. You'll be helping the farmer and letting yourself in for a real treat.

multicolor heirloom tomatoes with burrata and aged balsamic | *serves 4*

6 multicolored heirloom tomatoes or any good, ripe tomatoes
2 balls burrata cheese, 4 to 5 ounces each
$^1/4$ cup extra virgin olive oil
3 tablespoons aged balsamic vinegar
3 tablespoons torn fresh basil
Cracked black pepper

1. Core the tomatoes and slice $^1/2$ inch thick. Slice the cheese $^1/2$ inch thick.
2. Divide the tomato and cheese slices among 4 serving plates. Shingle them so the colors alternate: red, white, yellow, white, and so on.
3. Drizzle each plate with olive oil and vinegar, then garnish with basil and pepper.

about the wine

Podere Poggio Scalette in Tuscany produces "Il Carbanaione," a wine of legend and lore made from a clone of Sangiovese called Sangiovese di Lamole. The vines were planted in 1920, and the resulting wine is redolent of black fruits and herbs. It can diffuse the acidity of the tomatoes while enhancing the buttery cheese.

I developed this to commemorate the lobster diavolo my mother made on Christmas Eve when I was growing up. *Diavolo* means "devil" and is applied to the many variations of lobster diavolo because of the inherent heat in the tomato-based sauce. Cajuns also lay claim to a diavolo (sometimes called by its Spanish name, *diablo*) made with crayfish; theirs is served over rice, not the pasta that you find in Italian restaurants. I first made this with some gorgeous jumbo crawfish that arrived at Tru one day and have been making it ever since. I suppose you could say it is a marriage of the Cajun and the Italian, but I toss in a little Spanish influence with the piquillo peppers. But no tomatoes, pasta, or rice in sight. Just terrific flavor.

jumbo crawfish with diavolo vinaigrette | *serves 4*

4 jumbo crawfish, small lobsters, langoustines, or jumbo shrimp
    (about 2 pounds total; see Note)
$^1/_4$ cup red wine vinegar
1 orange, cut into 8 wedges
2 garlic cloves, minced
$^1/_2$ cup chopped piquillo peppers (see page 44) or roasted red peppers (see page 117)
2 tablespoons chopped fresh flat-leaf parsley, plus more for garnish
1 tablespoon chopped Calabrian chiles or $1^1/_2$ teaspoons crushed red pepper flakes
1 tablespoon chopped fresh chives
1 tablespoon torn fresh basil
$1^1/_2$ teaspoons chopped fresh oregano, plus more for garnish
Juice and grated zest of 1 lemon
1 cup olive oil
Orange slices

1.   Rinse the crawfish under cool running water. Put them in a steaming basket and set the basket over water in a stockpot. Cover and bring to a boil over high heat. Let the crawfish steam for 3 to 4 minutes, or until bright red. (If steaming shrimp, you might need less time, and if steaming lobster or langoustines, you might need a few minutes longer.) Remove from the steaming basket and set aside to cool until warm or room temperature. Transfer to a large bowl.

(continued)

2. In a mixing bowl, combine the vinegar, orange wedges, garlic, piquillo peppers, parsley, chiles, chives, basil, oregano, and lemon juice and zest. Whisk in the olive oil until emulsified.

3. Transfer to a saucepan and heat gently over medium heat until warm. Pour over the crawfish and toss to mix.

4. Put the steamed crawfish, including the orange wedges, on a platter. Garnish with orange slices, oregano, and parsley.

NOTE You can also boil the crawfish instead of steaming. Use a spice mixture designed for boiling crawfish or crabs and follow the directions on the package.

about the wine

If you like to drink red, Sangiovese can handle the spice factor here, and as mentioned at the beginning of this chapter, the grape appears in one of its many forms in the central regions of Italy. Long ago dismissed from the list of serious wine regions, the Marche is coming on strong with wines like Rosso Piceno, in which Sangiovese is paired with Montepulciano. Producers like Antonio Terni at Fattoria Le Terrazze and Cocci Griffoni are making strong statements with this style of wine.

My big Italian family lived near each other when I was a kid and every Sunday, rain or shine, we assembled after church for a family meal that would last all day. Along with the expected pasta course, there was always an eggplant parmesan. All resembled each other, with only slight variations, and I can't honestly say I preferred one to another.

When I traveled to Calabria in southern Italy, I ate a dish that reminded me of the eggplant parmesan of my childhood—but only slightly. I mean, it was over the top! This dish is an homage to the eggplant parmesans lovingly prepared by my mother, aunts, and grandmothers, as well as the incredible eggplant dish I discovered in Italy. Look for medium-sized rather than large eggplants, as they will be milder. By the way, when I was a child I never heard the word *eggplant*. Both grandmothers spoke only Italian and so I heard "melanzane" this and "melanzane" that. When I got out on my own, I heard myself asking, "What is an eggplant?" Imagine my surprise when I found out it was nothing more exotic than *melanzane!*

Caciocavallo cheese is a cow or buffalo milk cheese produced in southern Italy and not commonly found elsewhere. It's an unrefined cheese that is usually aged so that it's easy to slice. Its flavor is sharper than mozzarella but mozzarella is a good substitute.

eggplant calabrese | *serves 4 to 6*

4 pounds eggplant

Kosher salt

2 tablespoons all-purpose flour

Freshly ground black pepper

$^3/_4$ cup plus 2 tablespoons olive oil

$^1/_2$ cup chopped onion

2 tablespoons minced garlic

1 pound tomatoes, peeled

10 fresh basil leaves

1 bay leaf

1 sprig fresh thyme

$^1/_2$ pound ground beef

3 large eggs

3 tablespoons bread crumbs

2 tablespoons chopped fresh flat-leaf parsley, plus more for garnish

$^1/_2$ pound Caciocavallo or mozzarella cheese

2 hard-cooked large eggs

1 cup freshly grated Parmigiano-Reggiano cheese, plus more for garnish

1. Cut the eggplant into thin disks. Sprinkle with salt and put in a colander to drain for 30 to 40 minutes.
2. Rinse the eggplant under cold running water and pat dry with paper towels.
3. Spread the flour in a shallow dish and drag the eggplant through the flour to coat on both sides. Season with salt and pepper.
4. Preheat the oven to 400°F.
5. In a skillet, heat $1/2$ cup of the olive oil over medium heat and panfry the eggplant slices for 2 to 3 minutes on each side, or until very lightly browned. Drain on paper towels and set aside.
6. In a saucepan, heat 2 tablespoons of the remaining olive oil over medium heat. Add the onion and garlic and cook for 2 to 3 minutes, or until the onion softens.
7. Press the tomatoes through a sieve or food mill and add to the saucepan with the basil, bay leaf, thyme, and 2 tablespoons of the remaining oil. Season to taste with salt and pepper. Cook over low heat for 3 to 4 minutes, or until the tomatoes thicken. Remove the pan from the heat.
8. In a mixing bowl, combine the beef, eggs, bread crumbs, and parsley. Blend well and season with salt and pepper. Shape the beef into 8 flattened, oval croquettes.
9. In a sauté pan, heat the remaining 2 tablespoons of oil over medium-high heat. Cook the croquettes for 2 to 3 minutes on each side, or until they begin to brown. Drain on paper towels.
10. Thinly slice the Caciocavallo and slice the hard-cooked eggs.
11. Spread about a quarter of the tomato sauce over the bottom of an ovenproof dish large enough to hold half the eggplant in a single layer. Cover with half the eggplant slices and sprinkle with half of the Parmigiano-Reggiano. Layer the croquettes, the cheese slices, and then the egg slices. Cover with another quarter of the tomato sauce and the remaining eggplant slices. Sprinkle with the rest of the Parmigiano-Reggiano and another quarter of the sauce. Reserve the remaining sauce and keep it hot. Bake for 30 minutes, or until the casserole is set and the sauce is bubbling.
12. Cut squares of the eggplant casserole and put one on each of 4 serving plates. Spoon the remaining sauce over the eggplant and garnish with parsley and grated cheese.

about the wine

Magliocco and Gaglioppo, the two primary grape varietals of Calabria, are so fun to say. Delight your inner wine geek and serve these with the eggplant to your unsuspecting friends. Calabrian reds can be difficult to find but the rewards are great. These are hot-climate wines with all of the juiciness and jamminess that you can stand. We have loved the wines of Terre di Balbia.

Anyone who has read my other books knows how I feel about prosciutto di Parma, the heady, luxuriously fat-streaked ham from Parma, Italy. So it will come as no surprise to hear that I was in heaven (dare I say "hog heaven"?) when I walked into Il Latini, a restaurant in Florence dedicated to all manner of salumi and especially to prosciutto. In each of the restaurant's four large dining rooms hams hang from the ceiling like chandeliers, each slung with a small cup to catch any dripping fat. When you enter, the first thing you see is two guys slicing salumi with bright red, old-fashioned, hand-cranked deli slicers. I couldn't get enough of the prosciutto—the best I ever tasted. Of course, the entire experience was lots of fun. The restaurant is hidden away at the end of an alley and if not for the line forming outside at 4:30 P.M., I would have walked right by. And don't think of this as a tourist joint. The crowd is a reassuring mixture of locals and tourists.
Prosciutto di Parma comes from the same region famous for Parmigiano-Reggiano cheese and Ferrari automobiles. It's a classic, and one that will never let you down.

prosciutto di parma with three melons | *serves 4*

16 very thin slices prosciutto di Parma
4 teaspoons extra virgin olive oil
Cracked black pepper
16 balls honeydew melon, about the size of a walnut, scooped with a melon baller
Twelve 1-inch cubes seedless watermelon
Eight $^1/4$-inch-thick slices cantaloupe
1 tablespoon julienned fresh mint
1 tablespoon chestnut honey or other mild honey
Kosher salt

1. Lay 4 slices of prosciutto flat on each of 4 serving plates. Drizzle each plate with olive oil and sprinkle with cracked pepper.
2. In a mixing bowl, toss together the honeydew, watermelon, cantaloupe, mint, and honey. Season with a pinch of salt and toss gently.
3. Scatter the melon over the prosciutto and serve.

about the wine

Nothing makes us happier than a plate of prosciutto di Parma with melons and Prosecco—especially if it is a magnum of Nino Franco "Rustico" or a top offering from Bisol.

When I cooked on a Silver Seas Mediterranean cruise one year I had lunch at a beautiful seaside *enoteca* on Capri. Our table quickly filled up with little plates of delicious combinations of food, and the one that stayed with me was a thinly sliced, perfectly ripe avocado served with sea salt, fresh ground pepper, lemon juice, and amazing olive oil. I have spun this to make my own version. Make sure the olive oil is great and the avocados and pears are perfectly ripe.

Ricotta salata, originally from Sicily or Sardinia, is pure white sheep's-milk cheese. Sold in rounds, it is smooth, milky, and mildly sweet and nutty. It is not unlike feta cheese in its saltiness, which can be substituted for it, if necessary. Ricotta salata is becoming increasingly easy to find in American supermarkets and specialty stores, so keep a lookout for it.

avocado carpaccio with pears and ricotta salata | *serves 4*

$^1/_4$ cup sherry vinegar
Juice and grated zest of $^1/_2$ orange
$^1/_2$ cup extra virgin olive oil
1 teaspoon chopped fresh mint
1 teaspoon chopped fresh chives
Kosher salt and freshly ground black pepper
2 ripe avocados
2 cups assorted baby salad greens
2 ripe Forelle or Asian pears, cored and peeled
$^2/_3$ cup ricotta salata cheese

1. In a small bowl, whisk together the vinegar, orange juice, and zest. Slowly whisk in the olive oil until the vinaigrette emulsifies. Stir in the mint and chives and season to taste with salt and pepper. Set aside.
2. Peel the avocados, remove the pits, and slice the fruit as thinly as possible. Shingle the slices on each of 4 serving plates.
3. Slice the pears as thinly as possible.
4. Put the greens in a small bowl and add the pear slices. Dress with $^1/_4$ cup of the vinaigrette and toss.

5.   Pile the salad on top of the avocados and drizzle with a little more vinaigrette. Crumble the ricotta salata over the salad and serve.

about the wine

Perfectly ripe, silky avocados need a similarly textured wine, and the ricotta salata demands one that can handle, as the name implies, a salty flavor. The white wine made from the Falanghina grape in Campania, called simply Falanghina, to the rescue!

This humble yet tasty little offering is straight from the Tramonto family culinary lineage. I know this was passed down to my mother from my grandmother, and to her from my great-grandmother; I grew up eating escarole and beans, escarole and sausage, escarole and garlic . . . you name it! When young, escarole leaves can be eaten raw in salads, but more commonly they are lightly cooked like other greens. In Italian households, escarole is added to soups, pasta dishes, and risottos, and served as a side dish. As many of us feel about the simple dishes from our childhoods, I find this incredibly soothing and homey. And despite the long list of ingredients, it's very easy to make.

sautéed escarole and cannellini beans | *serves 4*

$^1/_2$ cup olive oil

1 cup diced bacon

2 celery ribs, diced

1 onion, diced

1 carrot, diced

3 garlic cloves, chopped

1 tablespoon crushed red pepper flakes

1 bay leaf

6 cups chopped escarole (about 2-inch pieces)

6 cups Cooked Cannellini Beans (page 93)

2 cups canned crushed tomatoes

$^2/_3$ cup white wine

1 quart chicken stock

2 tablespoons freshly grated Parmigiano-Reggiano cheese, plus $^1/_4$ cup shaved

Kosher salt and freshly ground black pepper

2 tablespoons unsalted butter

Extra virgin olive oil, for drizzling

2 tablespoons torn fresh basil

2 tablespoons chopped fresh flat-leaf parsley

1. In a heavy pot, heat the olive oil over medium-high heat. Add the bacon, celery, onion, carrot, garlic, red pepper, and bay leaf and sauté for 5 to 7 minutes, or until the onion is lightly browned.

2. Stir in the escarole and sauté for 2 minutes. Add the beans, cook for 2 to 3 minutes, then add the tomatoes, stir, and cook about 2 minutes longer.

3. Add the wine and deglaze, scraping the bottom of the pan and cooking for 2 to 3 minutes. Add the chicken stock and bring to a boil, then reduce the heat and simmer briskly for 5 to 7 minutes, or until reduced by half. Stir in the grated cheese and season to taste with salt and black pepper. Add the butter and stir until incorporated.

4. Divide the beans among 4 bowls. Drizzle with olive oil, sprinkle with the basil, parsley, and shaved cheese, and serve.

about the wine

Not many Italian wines are more soothing than a bottle of perfectly aged Sangiovese in the guise of Brunello di Montalcino. It's a wine that is renowned for its ability to improve for decades. With time, this wine, which can be monstrous when young, matures into a supple, complex creature with length and distinction. Got a bottle from the legendary producer Biondi-Santi? Cin cin!

homemade cannellini beans | makes about 6 cups

1 pound dried cannellini beans
2 sprigs fresh thyme
1 bay leaf
$1^1/2$ teaspoons black peppercorns

1. Put the dried beans in a bowl or pot and add enough cold water to cover. Set aside to soak at room temperature for at least 8 hours. Change the water once or twice, if possible.

2. Drain the beans and transfer to a heavy-bottomed pot.

3. Wrap the thyme, bay leaf, and peppercorns in a double thickness of cheesecloth. Tie the cheesecloth into a bundle and add to the pot. Add water to cover by an inch or two.

4. Bring the water to a boil over high heat. Reduce the heat to medium-low, skim off any foam that rises to the surface, and simmer 40 to 50 minutes, until the beans are al dente. Check the water level during cooking and replenish it, if necessary. It's important to keep the beans submerged at all times during cooking.

5. Drain the beans and discard the herb bundle. Cool the beans at room temperature, then cover and refrigerate until needed. The cooked beans will keep for up to 2 days.

When you indulge in fresh truffles, a relatively small financial investment yields a big payoff in terms of flavor. There's no denying that the luxurious fungi are pricey, but even a few infuse the butter for these potatoes with rich, earthy perfume. I was inspired to create this dish one autumn after I went truffle hunting in the Piedmont hills of Italy with a guide named Luigi and some dogs trained to sniff out the treasures. In the old days, pigs were used to unearth the truffles, but these days, dogs do the job. If you are fortunate enough to be in Italy in truffle season, you can pretty much go into any restaurant and expect to see a balance scale on the table. The waiter puts a fresh-dug truffle on the scale and sets a truffle slicer next to it; you shave as much truffle as you want over the pasta or anything else. At the end of the meal, you are charged for the weight of the truffle you have consumed. Buyer beware: Seven-euro pasta dishes can easily turn into 70- or even 700-euro meals!

salted fingerling potatoes and truffle butter | *serves 4*

8 fingerling potatoes

$^1/4$ cup olive oil

Kosher salt and cracked black pepper

$^1/2$ pound (2 sticks) unsalted butter, softened

$^1/4$ cup truffle oil

Chopped fresh black or white truffles (as many as you can afford) or $^1/4$ cup canned truffles, plus shaved truffles for garnish, optional

Juice of $^1/2$ lemon

$^1/4$ cup freshly grated Parmigiano-Reggiano cheese

2 tablespoons chopped fresh chives

1 tablespoon chopped fresh flat-leaf parsley

1. Preheat the oven to 400°F.
2. In a bowl, toss the potatoes with the olive oil and salt and pepper to taste. Spread the potatoes in a baking pan and roast for 40 to 50 minutes, until tender when pierced with a fork.
3. Meanwhile, in the bowl of an electric mixer, fitted with the paddle attachment, beat the butter, truffle oil, chopped truffles and lemon juice on medium speed until well mixed. Season to taste with salt and pepper.

4. Lay a piece of plastic wrap on the countertop and scrape the truffle butter onto the center. Wrap the butter in the plastic.

5. Remove the potatoes from the oven and cut a lengthwise slit in each potato. Pinch the ends of the potatoes so the slit opens.

6. Top each potato with a teaspoon of truffle butter, some cheese, chives, parsley, and shaved truffles, if desired. Refrigerate or freeze the butter you don't use.

about the wine

The earthy style of Brunello, beautiful black fruited wines made from Sangiovese, echo the earthy flavors of the truffle, and there are many outstanding producers to choose from. Some of our favorites include Gaja's "Sugarille," La Fiorita, Ciacci Piccolomini d'Aragona, and Livio Sassetti.

I have always loved mustard on everything, from steaks to sandwiches. For years now I have made mustards and "customized" others with all sorts of good things, as I do here by adding almond oil and lemon juice to a good coarse-grained mustard. It's great with meat, especially speck, which is just spicy and smoky enough to stand up to it. I suggest this with blood oranges, one of my favorite fruits of all time; they come into season in the wintertime when their bright color and sweet juiciness are very welcome. I know I am in Italy when I get to order blood orange juice for breakfast!

speck with blood oranges and almond mustard | *serves 4*

2 blood oranges, peeled
$^1/4$ cup olive oil
1 cup shaved celery (see Note)
1 cup shaved fennel (see Note)
1 tablespoon torn fresh basil
Kosher salt and cracked black pepper
$^1/2$ cup stone-ground mustard or other coarse-grained mustard
2 tablespoons almond oil, plus more if needed
2 tablespoons fresh lemon juice, plus more if needed
16 thin slices speck (see Note)

1. Working above a bowl, segment the oranges, letting any juice drip into the bowl. Set aside the segments. Whisk in the olive oil.
2. Add the celery and fennel to the bowl, along with the orange segments and basil. Season to taste with salt and pepper.
3. In another small bowl, whisk the mustard with the almond oil and lemon juice. Taste and add a little more oil or juice, if necessary.
4. Lay 4 slices of speck on each of 4 serving plates. Mound the orange salad in the center of each plate on top of the speck. Spoon the mustard on the plate or serve it on the side.

NOTE Shave very thin pieces of celery and fennel. Use a mandoline, if possible, for the thinnest pieces. Speck is cured Italian ham, similar to prosciutto but cut from the leg of the hog and cured with flavors such as beechwood and juniper. It is both spicy and smoky and is served in the same way as prosciutto. (German speck is made from lard and is used like bacon; do not confuse it with Italian speck.)

about the wine

The Lungarotti family is credited with putting Umbrian wines on the map, and every time we drink a glass of their "Rubesco," which is fairly often, we tip our hats to them. "Rubesco" is classified as a Rosso di Torgiano; this blend of Sangiovese and Caniolo has the perfect amount of finesse so as not to fight with the sweet blood orange and the bitter almond.

This bocconcini stuck in my head after I tasted a similar dish at Trattoria Masuelli in Milan, a small family-run restaurant with about thirty seats. When you eat there, you almost feel as though you are sitting at your grandma's table. The mushrooms literally had been foraged by the owner just a few hours earlier, and the salumi was served on a small cutting board so you could slice it at the table. And the cheese? So appealingly crumbly and heady, I was blown away by it!

grilled porcini mushrooms with crumbled
sottobosco cheese | *serves 4*

2 pounds fresh porcini mushrooms
$1/4$ cup extra virgin olive oil, plus more for brushing
Kosher salt and cracked black pepper
2 cups arugula
4 beefsteak tomatoes, cored and chopped
Juice of $1/2$ lemon
2 tablespoons chopped fresh basil
1 tablespoon chopped fresh flat-leaf parsley
$1/4$ cup crumbled Sottobosco cheese (see Note)
4 teaspoons truffle oil, optional

1. Prepare a gas or charcoal grill. The heating elements or coals should be medium-hot.
2. Peel the caps from the mushrooms and discard the peelings. Trim the stems and then brush the mushrooms clean. Slice 1 inch thick, brush with olive oil, and season with salt and pepper.
3. Grill the mushroom slices for 2 to 3 minutes on each side, just until they darken a little.
4. Meanwhile, put the arugula and tomatoes in a mixing bowl and dress with the $1/4$ cup of olive oil and the lemon juice. Add the basil and parsley, toss, and season to taste with salt and pepper.
5. Divide the mushrooms among 4 serving plates. Top with the salad and crumble the cheese over the salad. Drizzle with truffle oil, if desired.

NOTE Sottobosco cheese, also called Bianco Sottobosco, is handmade from cow's and goat's milk and mixed with sliced black Italian truffles. Made in the Piedmont region of Italy, Sottobosco is not well known anywhere else in the world, although you can sometimes find it in good cheese shops or buy it on the Internet. I love it and so make the effort to secure some wherever and however I can. An aged cheese, it's dry and crumbly and delightfully perfumed with truffles. It is most often served crumbled on top of salad, as in this recipe, or on a cheese board. If you can't find it, substitute another aged, dry, crumbly goat's-milk cheese.

about the wine

The Sangiovese-based Chiantis from the northernmost part of the region earn the special designation Chianti Rufina. Cool-climate viticulture is at work in this region, considered the most superior growing area in Chianti. Firm acidity, assertive bouquet, and elegant flavors characterize these wines, whose fruit and earthy character will pair well with the mushrooms and earthy Sottobosco cheese. Try Chianti Rufina from Selvapiana and Colognole.

Most of the recipes in this book are inspired by two things: my childhood, growing up in a very Italian family in upstate New York; and my travels through Italy as a chef. This dish falls into the former category, although the presentation is now more elegant and "cheflike." My aunts made awesome savory cheese casseroles in white Corning Ware baking dishes that we ate like puddings. They tasted very much like these flans, although because I use Grana Padano cheese and serve a little orange and frisée salad alongside them, this dish is more refined. What can I say? It's the chef in me!

grana padano flan with basil olive oil | *serves 6*

2 large eggs
4 ounces freshly grated Grana Padano cheese, plus 3 ounces shaved (see Note)
Juice and grated zest of 1 orange
1 teaspoon kosher salt
$^1/_4$ teaspoon freshly ground black pepper
Pinch of freshly grated nutmeg
2 cups heavy cream
$^1/_4$ cup olive oil
3 cups torn frisée
1 orange, peeled and segmented
1 tablespoon chopped fresh chives
3 tablespoons Basil Oil (page 101)
3 ounces Grana Padano cheese, shaved

1. Preheat the oven to 275°F. Butter six 8-ounce ceramic ramekins, glass custard cups, or disposable aluminum cups.
2. In the bowl of a food processor fitted with the metal blade, combine the eggs, grated cheese, orange zest (reserve the juice to use later), salt, pepper, and nutmeg. Process for about 3 minutes. Add the cream and process for 30 seconds or until smooth.
3. Divide the flan mixture among the ramekins and set them in a roasting pan or baking dish. Put the pan on the center rack of the oven and pour in enough hot water to come halfway up the sides of the ramekins.
4. Bake for 30 minutes. Reduce the heat to 200°F, and bake for 10 to 15 minutes longer, until the centers of the flans are firm to the touch.
5. Remove the pan from the oven and let the flans cool in the water for about 10 minutes.

6.   Meanwhile, in a mixing bowl, whisk together the olive oil and reserved orange juice; season to taste with salt and pepper. Add the frisée, orange segments, and chives and toss to mix.

7.   Set a small serving plate face down over each flan and, holding securely, invert the flan onto the plate. Spoon about $^1/_2$ cup of the orange and frisée salad next to each flan. Drizzle each flan with Basil Oil and garnish with the shaved cheese.

NOTE Grana Padano is an excellent grating cheese made in a similar manner to Parmigiano-Reggiano, however, it's aged for only half a year, as opposed to one to four years. It's less expensive, too, and for this reason has been called the "poor man's Parmesan." The word *grana* means "granular" and is a generic term for any cheese made in this style.

about the wine

The required wine for this textural delight with a punch of green is Franciacorta rosé. We are addicted to pink sparkling wines with good reason: they are great with food. Bellavista is a perennial award winner for its elegant, flavorful, traditionally produced wines. The nutty notes from the cheese are echoed by the toasty, leesy notes from the wine. Cool.

basil oil | makes about $^3/_4$ cup

$^1/_2$ cup extra virgin olive oil
$^1/_2$ cup fresh basil leaves
Kosher salt and freshly ground black pepper

1.   In a blender, combine the olive oil and basil and blend until emulsified. Season with salt and pepper and blend again.

2.   Strain through a fine-mesh sieve into a lidded container. Cover and refrigerate until needed.

If you like tripe, which falls into the category of offal and is the muscular lining of a cow's stomach, you will want to try this. All my aunts—and there were six of them!—cooked tripe when I was growing up, and all did so very well, but that never stopped the whispering and sly winks about who made the best tripe and who made the best calamari pie! In my opinion, Aunt Dorothy Tramonto's tripe was best, although I never turned down the offerings of the other aunts. As does Dorothy, I like to use white honeycomb tripe for this recipe; cut from the second of the cow's four stomachs, it is especially tender and light. Tripe has its own distinctive aroma, which greets you the minute you walk in the door. It makes those of us who savor it very happy! Still, I have never matched my aunt Dorothy when it comes to cooking tripe. She is the best.

aunt dorothy's tripe with
spicy tomato sauce | *serves 4 to 6*

TRIPE

5 pounds white honeycomb tripe

3 cups good-quality red wine vinegar

3 tablespoons kosher salt

SAUCE

$^1/_2$ cup olive oil

6 garlic cloves, minced

1 cup diced onion

1 cup diced celery

1 tablespoon crushed red pepper flakes

2 cups red wine

Two 28-ounce cans crushed tomatoes

One 6-ounce can tomato paste

1 bay leaf

Kosher salt and cracked black pepper

$^1/_3$ cup freshly grated Parmigiano-Reggiano cheese

1 tablespoon chopped fresh basil

1 tablespoon chopped fresh flat-leaf parsley

Extra virgin olive oil

1. *To prepare the tripe:* Remove the excess pockets of fat from the tripe and put the tripe, all in one piece, in a large stockpot. Add enough cold water to cover, 1 cup of the vinegar, and 1 tablespoon of salt.

2. Bring to a boil over medium-high heat. As soon as the water comes to a boil, remove from the heat and drain in a colander. Rinse well with cold running water.

3. Return the tripe to the pot and add the same amount of water, vinegar, and salt. Repeat the boiling, draining, and rinsing procedure. Repeat a third time.

4. Lay the drained and rinsed tripe on a perforated or wire rack set in a pan, cover with plastic wrap, and refrigerate for at least 8 hours and up to 12 hours to dry out thoroughly.

5. *To make the sauce:* Heat the oil over medium heat in a deep sauté pan. Sauté the garlic, onion, celery, and red pepper for 3 to 4 minutes or until the onion is translucent. Add the red wine and bring to a brisk simmer, scraping the bottom of the pan with a wooden spoon to deglaze.

6. Add the tomatoes, tomato paste, and bay leaf. Stir well and season to taste with salt and black pepper.

7. Remove the tripe from the refrigerator and cut it into strips as wide as your pinky finger. Transfer the strips to the sauce and simmer for 30 to 45 minutes, until the tripe is tender.

8. Ladle the tripe and sauce into 4 bowls. Garnish with grated cheese, basil, parsley, and a drizzle of extra virgin olive oil. If you have leftovers, refrigerate for up to 2 days.

about the wine

This dish is a no-holds-barred onslaught of meaty flavors. When choosing a wine to enjoy with it, adopt the same tactic. Tenimenti D'Alessandro's "Il Bosco" Syrah from Cortona on the eastern border of Tuscany is considered one of the best examples of Syrah in Italy. With its palate of rich, dark fruit and black pepper, "Il Bosco" will go head-to-head with Aunt Dorothy's tripe.

I love eggs with ham, and this is my take on one of the best ways to play on the concept. You cannot get much more Italian than this bocconcini. I first tasted something similar at Cibreo, a restaurant, *trattoria,* and bar run by Fabio Picchi in Florence, where the food is traditionally Tuscan. It's very simple to prepare, but you might be put off by the raw egg yolks drizzled over the meat. If you think of the flavors that are matched with the eggs—olive oil, lemon juice, and salty cheese—this little plate makes all kinds of sense. If you are still uncomfortable with the raw yolks, coddle the eggs first (cook them in boiling water for one minute) or lightly poach them. Look for organic eggs, too.

bresaola with egg yolk and parmesan | *serves 4*

3/4 pound bresaola, thinly sliced
Extra virgin olive oil
2 large egg yolks
1/2 teaspoon chopped fresh oregano
Cracked black pepper
Juice of 1 lemon
1/2 cup shaved Parmigiano-Reggiano cheese

1. Divide the bresaola among 4 serving plates. Drizzle with olive oil.
2. In a small bowl, beat the egg yolks until smooth. Drizzle over the bresaola. Sprinkle a little oregano over each plate and season to taste with pepper.
3. Drizzle lemon juice over each plate and garnish with cheese.

about the wine

When eating a Tuscan classic, do as the Tuscans do, and drink the local red. The wine region called the Maremma is where the innovators of the Tuscan wine scene are centered. In the southerly reaches, they are making Morellino di Scansano and other dark, rich, powerful reds from Sangiovese, Cabernet Sauvignon, Merlot, and similar grapes. We love to drink the Morellino from Fattoria Pupille with this dish.

A clean, fresh-tasting summery salad with lots of satisfying crunch and bright flavor, this is a winner. Ceci beans, which are also called chickpeas and garbanzo beans, were a staple in my house when I was growing up. My mom, Gloria, made pasta fagiole, the homestyle pasta-and-bean soup that Italian home cooks have been making for generations, for the whole neighborhood, but she also tossed cooked ceci beans into salads and vegetable dishes. They are a great sponge for other flavors, especially lemon and olive oil.

ceci bean, shaved celery, and cabbage salad | *serves 4*

CHAMPAGNE VINAIGRETTE
^{1}/4 cup Champagne vinegar
Juice of ^{1}/2 lemon
1 teaspoon lemon zest
1 cup extra virgin olive oil
1 teaspoon crushed red pepper flakes
Kosher salt and freshly ground black pepper

SALAD
2 cups Cooked Ceci Beans (page 106)
2 cups thinly sliced Napa cabbage
1 cup shaved celery
^{1}/4 cup thinly sliced scallions, green parts only
^{1}/2 red bell pepper, julienned
^{1}/2 yellow bell pepper, julienned
1 tablespoon chopped fresh flat-leaf parsley
1 tablespoon chopped fresh tarragon
Kosher salt and freshly ground black pepper

1. *To make the vinaigrette:* Combine the vinegar, lemon juice, and zest in a blender. With the motor running, slowly add the olive oil until the vinaigrette emulsifies. Add the red pepper and season to taste with salt and black pepper. Transfer to a storage container or glass jar, cover, and refrigerate until needed, for up to 2 days.

(continued)

2. *To make the salad:* In a mixing bowl, toss together the beans, cabbage, celery, scallions, bell peppers, parsley, and tarragon. Season to taste with salt and pepper.

3. Add enough vinaigrette to dress well. You will need between $^1/_2$ and $^3/_4$ cup. Reserve any leftover vinaigrette for another use.

4. Divide the salad among 4 serving plates or pile it high on a platter.

about the wine

While the creamy ceci beans may be able to handle a red wine, this dish has many detractors to that plan, such as the high-acid components: Champagne vinegar and lemon. Keep your wine choice fresh and clean. Crisp, lean Müller-Thurgau from a producer like Pojer e Sandri in Trentino will stay in theme.

homemade ceci beans | makes about 5 cups

2 cups dried ceci beans (also called chickpeas and garbanzo beans)
1 carrot, peeled and cut in large chunks
1 onion, peeled and cut in large chunks
1 bay leaf
1 sprig fresh thyme
$^1/_2$ teaspoon crushed red pepper flakes
Kosher salt and freshly ground black pepper

1. Put the dried beans in a bowl or pot and add enough cold water to cover. Set aside to soak in the refrigerator for 24 hours. Change the water once or twice, if possible.

2. Drain the beans, transfer to a heavy-bottomed pot, and add the carrot, onion, bay leaf, thyme, and red pepper. Season with salt and black pepper. Add water to cover by an inch or two.

3. Bring the water to a boil over high heat. Reduce the heat to medium-low, skim off any foam that rises to the surface, and simmer for about 1 hour, or until the beans are tender. Check the water level during cooking and replenish it, if necessary. It's important to keep the beans submerged at all times during cooking.

4. Drain the beans and discard the vegetables and herbs. Cool the beans at room temperature, then cover and refrigerate until needed. The cooked beans will keep for up to 2 days.

One of my good friends, Chef David DiGregorio of Osteria Via Stato in Chicago, shared a version of this recipe with me, explaining that it was part of his family's culinary traditions. From the minute I tasted the little meatballs, I was hooked. While I think they are great with caramelized onions, you could serve them with tomato sauce or spooned over pasta. Either way, they are *fantastico*!

mini veal meatballs with
caramelized onions | *serves 4 to 6*

ONIONS

2 tablespoons olive oil

2 garlic cloves, chopped

2 cups thinly sliced onions

1 tablespoon sugar

Kosher salt and freshly ground black pepper

$^1/_2$ cup red wine

1 bay leaf

1 tablespoon chopped fresh thyme

1 quart chicken stock, or 2 cups chicken stock and 2 cups veal stock

2 tablespoons unsalted butter

2 tablespoons aged balsamic vinegar

MEATBALLS

2 cups panko (Japanese bread crumbs) or other coarse dried crumbs

8 tablespoons (1 stick) unsalted butter, melted and slightly cooled

1 cup freshly grated Parmigiano-Reggiano cheese

1 cup whole milk

3 large eggs, lightly beaten

2 tablespoons finely minced garlic

2 tablespoons chopped fresh flat-leaf parsley

1 tablespoon chopped fresh oregano

1 tablespoon olive oil

1 tablespoon kosher salt

1 tablespoon freshly ground black pepper

1 teaspoon crushed red pepper flakes

1 teaspoon finely grated lemon zest

$^1/_2$ pound ground pork
$^1/_2$ pound ground veal
1 tomato, coarsely diced
1 tablespoon julienned fresh basil

1. *To make the onions:* Heat the olive oil in a large saucepan over medium-high heat. Add the garlic, onions, and sugar; season with salt and pepper; and cook, stirring occasionally, for 10 to 15 minutes, until caramelized and golden brown.
2. Add the wine, bay leaf, and thyme. Bring to a boil, then reduce the heat and simmer briskly for 3 to 6 minutes or until reduced by half. Add the stock and bring to a boil, then reduce the heat and simmer briskly for 5 to 8 minutes, or until reduced by half.
3. Stir the butter into the sauce and when it's incorporated, season to taste with salt and pepper. Finish with a splash of vinegar (1 to 2 teaspoons). Cover and keep warm.
4. *To make the meatballs:* Preheat the oven to 350°F. Lightly oil a baking sheet.
5. In a large mixing bowl, combine the bread crumbs and melted butter and mix well by hand. Add the cheese, milk, eggs, 1 tablespoon of the parsley, the oregano, olive oil, salt, black and red pepper, and lemon zest and mix well.
6. Add the ground pork and veal to the bowl and mix well.
7. Pinch off small walnut-sized pieces of meat, each about $^1/_2$ ounce, and make mini meatballs. You should have between 32 and 40 meatballs. A few extra are fine.
8. Transfer the meatballs to the baking sheet. Arrange them in neat rows, leaving space between them.
9. Bake for 10 to 12 minutes, or until the meatballs are cooked through. Do not overcook. Divide the meatballs among 4 serving plates. Spoon the warm sauce over the top of the meatballs and garnish each plate with some of the remaining parsley, a little diced tomato, and basil. Drizzle the remaining vinegar over each plate and serve.

about the wine

The gently rolling hills of Montepulciano in Tuscany are the setting for the Sangiovese vineyards that produce Vino Nobile di Montepulciano. Generally earlier drinking than Brunello, and with lower acidity than Chianti, this category of wine is one of many that are wonderful with the veal meatballs. Well-balanced dishes need well-balanced wines, so try elegant examples from Avignonesi or Il Macchione.

CHAPTER 5

bruschetta

grilled bread
with robust toppings

The
term *bruschetta* trips off the lips of
most Americans with great familiarity, and I
couldn't be happier. What's not to like about a thick piece
of grilled Italian bread seasoned with olive oil and topped with
chopped tomatoes, onions, basil, and mozzarella cheese? Absolutely
nothing, except this is not a precise definition of *bruschetta*, although it describes
a common type served in restaurants. The word simply means a grilled piece of
bread, usually rubbed with garlic and drizzled with olive oil. It may or may not be
topped with some blissful blending of foods. In lean times, making bruschetta was a tasty
way to use day-old bread. I am sure Italian home cooks, who probably topped the slightly
stale bread with other leftovers, never dreamed the open-faced sandwich would one day be the
darling of American restaurants!
When you make bruschetta, size counts. The bread slices are relatively large and thick and topped
with hearty fillings that can stand up to the bread. They are grilled, not toasted, although it would
not be 100 percent wrong to do so, and embellished with grated cheese. In my world, there's
nothing dainty about a bruschetta. While they belong in a book about small plates, these are far
from small bites! From a spicy bean paste generously spread over the bread, to marinated skirt
steak, grilled just until nicely charred and garnished with an energetic arugula salad, these
toppings are instead the stuff of small but filling meals. When you serve one, two, or more
of Tramonto's bruschetta with several bottles of wine, you have a party!

ABOUT THE WINE
In the Italian wine hierarchy, Barolo and Barbaresco are indisputably king and queen.
The first two wines to be elevated to the vaunted Italian DOCG status, these
serious reds crafted from the Nebbiolo grape provide endless
deliciousness to wine-drinking thrill seekers. There is no
bruschetta that wouldn't love to be served with
one of these royal reds!

This is the ultimate vehicle for any number of toppings. The quality of the bread, as well as the olive oil, makes all the difference, so make sure the crust is crisp and the middle is soft and chewy. Buy it fresh from a good bakery. This is an example of two ingredients making the difference between good and truly great. Enjoy the ride!

rick's basic bruschetta | *serves 4*

Four $^1/_2$-inch-thick slices sourdough or any Italian country-style bread
$^1/_4$ cup olive oil
Kosher salt and freshly ground black pepper
1 garlic clove
1 tablespoon freshly grated Parmigiano-Reggiano cheese

1. Prepare a gas or charcoal grill or preheat the broiler or a panini press. The heating elements or coals should be medium-hot.
2. Cut the slices in half and brush both sides with a generous amount of olive oil. Season both sides with salt and pepper.
3. Grill or broil the bread, turning once, until lightly browned on both sides.
4. Gently rub 1 side of the toasts with garlic, sprinkle with cheese, and serve.

about the wine

This dish is a study in keeping it simple, so the big B's seem too fancy here. Opt instead for Piedmont's other delicious B-word: Barbera. As the most-planted red wine grape varietal in the region, Barbera represents the everyday, low-commitment version of Piedmontese red. Choose a no-frills version of this high-toned red, and stay away from fancy blends surrounded by quotes and anything that says "superiore."

Pecorino cheeses are crafted throughout much of Italy. My all-time favorites are the pecorinos made in Tuscany, particularly the cheeses from near the town of Pienza. *Pecora* is the Italian word for sheep, and these sheep's milk cheeses have a lovely yet intense flavor when aged for at least six months. You can cube the cheese and store it, covered with fruity olive oil, to eat as a snack. Amazing. But here, I shave the cheese over shaved green and white asparagus spears for an astounding bruschetta.

bruschetta with shaved white and green asparagus and pecorino toscano | *serves 4*

8 green asparagus spears
8 white asparagus spears
$^1/_4$ cup olive oil
1 tablespoon fresh lemon juice
1 tablespoon chopped fresh tarragon
1 tablespoon torn fresh basil
Kosher salt and cracked black pepper
8 slices Rick's Basic Bruschetta (page 112)
2 ounces pecorino Toscano cheese, shaved
Grated lemon zest

1. Bring a large saucepan of salted water to a boil. Cook the asparagus for 4 to 6 minutes, or until al dente. Drain, submerge in ice water to shock, and drain again.
2. When cook, using a potato peeler, shave the entire length of the asparagus spears, tips included, until all are cut into thin shavings.
3. In a nonreactive bowl, whisk together the olive oil, lemon juice, tarragon, and basil. Season to taste with salt and pepper, add the shaved asparagus, and toss gently.
4. Pile the asparagus mixture on top of the bruschetta, garnish with the pecorino and lemon zest, and serve.

about the wine

Barbera Vivace is a lesser-known style of almost sparkling Barbera that results from fermenting the grapes under pressure and trapping some of the resulting carbon dioxide in the wine. Intended to be served slightly chilled, Viberti makes a fruity, grapey style that is fun to try here.

For me, this bruschetta can only mean Rome! I recall a small *trattoria* in Vatican City that I stumbled upon after hearing Pope John Paul speak in Vatican Square. I was with my culinary partner, pastry chef Gale Gand, and we both ordered a few things. We sampled some wonderful bruschetta, including one with shaved fennel, big green Italian olives, and lots of great olive oil. I couldn't resist recreating it. Mine has a little orange juice and grated zest and is finished with a pinch of fennel pollen. Can't find fennel pollen? Don't let that stop you from trying this.

bruschetta with fennel and green olives | *serves 4*

2 bulbs fennel and 1 tablespoon chopped fronds

$^1/_2$ cup olive oil

1 tablespoon unsalted butter

2 garlic cloves, slivered

1 teaspoon crushed red pepper flakes

Juice and grated zest of 1 orange

$^1/_2$ teaspoon freshly grated nutmeg

2 cups arugula

1 cup large green olives, such as Cerignola, pitted and halved, or other
     high-quality large green olive

1 tablespoon sherry vinegar

Kosher salt and cracked black pepper

1 tablespoon torn fresh basil

8 slices Rick's Basic Bruschetta (page 112)

Pinch of fennel pollen

1. Cut the fennel bulbs lengthwise into $^3/_4$-inch slices.
2. Bring a saucepan of lightly salted water to a boil. Cook the fennel for 10 to 12 minutes, or until tender. Drain and set aside.
3. In a sauté pan, heat $^1/_4$ cup of the olive oil and the butter over medium heat. When the butter melts, cook the garlic and red pepper, stirring, for 2 to 3 minutes, until the garlic is lightly browned.
4. Add the fennel, orange juice and zest, and nutmeg. Raise the heat and simmer the orange juice briskly for 3 to 5 minutes, or until reduced to a glaze. Set aside to cool to room temperature.

5. In a small bowl, mix the arugula and olives and drizzle with the remaining olive oil and the sherry. Toss and season to taste with salt and black pepper.
6. Put a few slices of glazed fennel on top of each bruschetta. Top with the olive and arugula salad, garnish with the fennel fronds and a little fennel pollen, and serve.

about the wine

The dominant citrus notes from the orange and the spike of brown spice from the nutmeg in this bruschetta put us in the mood for a glass (or a bottle) of Roero Arneis, one of Piedmont's classic dry white wines. The Roero Arneis grape is known for producing high-toned, citrus-laced whites that often finish with a nutty note. Almondo is one of our favorite producers of this style of wine.

As I mentioned in Chapter 2, Italian white anchovies are milder and less salty than other canned anchovies and I highly recommend them to anyone—even if you firmly believe you "hate anchovies!" I have had this combination of roasted peppers and white anchovies in most Italian cities, from Florence to Venice to Milan, and have had it with and without bread. I like it as bruschetta with great olive oil—lots of it!

bruschetta with roasted peppers and white anchovies | *serves 4*

3 roasted yellow bell peppers (see Note)
3 roasted red bell peppers (see Note)
$^1/2$ cup extra virgin olive oil
2 garlic cloves, minced
2 tablespoons torn fresh basil
1 tablespoon drained, chopped capers
1 tablespoon chopped fresh flat-leaf parsley
2 teaspoons chopped Calabrian chiles or 1 teaspoon
    crushed red pepper flakes, optional
Kosher salt and cracked black pepper
8 slices Rick's Basic Bruschetta (page 112)
16 white anchovy fillets, drained (I prefer Medusa brand)
Juice of $^1/2$ lemon

1. Cut each pepper in half and remove the seeds and stems. Lay the halves flat and cut lengthwise into 6 to 8 strips. Transfer to a mixing bowl.
2. Add the olive oil, garlic, basil, capers, and parsley. Toss and add the chiles, if desired. Season to taste with salt and black pepper.
3. Top each bruschetta with the pepper mixture. Lay 2 anchovy fillets on top of each one, drizzle with lemon juice and the oil remaining in the bowl, and serve.

NOTE To roast bell peppers, char them over a grill or gas flame or under a broiler until blackened on all sides and soft. Turn them as they char to ensure even blackening. Remove from the heat and transfer to a bowl. Cover with plastic wrap and set aside for about 20 minutes to steam as they cool. Lift the peppers from the bowl and rub or peel off the blackened skin.

about the wine

We don't agree with the outdated axiom "drink white wine with fish, red wine with meat." It's all about balance. The little sweet one, Dolcetto, is a fun wine to drink with this presentation of salty white anchovies and sweet, roasted peppers. Fruity styles from producers like Boroli and Giacosa will surprise you with their ability to handle the flavors on this bruschetta.

The first time my wife, Eileen, tasted this bruschetta, she was surprised at how well zucchini and mint married. I trust her because she acts as my "weird radar"; she can always tell if something tastes as good as I think it does. On the other hand, I was not surprised in the least. My grandfather grew both in his garden and he frequently finished sautéed zucchini with a little fresh mint. We ate this for lunch with crusty bread, so I naturally thought of it for bruschetta.

bruschetta with roasted minted zucchini and fontina val d'aosta | *serves 4*

2 zucchini
$^{1}/4$ cup extra virgin olive oil, plus more for drizzling
2 garlic cloves, minced
1 shallot, minced
1 teaspoon crushed red pepper flakes
1 bay leaf
1 sprig fresh rosemary
Juice of $^{1}/2$ lemon
1 cup grated Fontina Val d'Aosta cheese (see Note)
8 slices Rick's Basic Bruschetta (page 112)
1 tablespoon chopped fresh mint

1. Preheat the oven to 400°F.
2. With a sharp knife or mandoline, cut the zucchini lengthwise into $^{1}/4$-inch-thick slices. Transfer to a bowl and add the $^{1}/4$ cup of olive oil, garlic, shallot, red pepper, bay leaf, and rosemary and toss to mix.
3. Spread the zucchini mixture in a small baking pan and roast for 20 to 25 minutes, until crisp and golden brown. Stir occasionally.
4. Remove from the oven but do not turn off the heat. Discard the bay leaf and rosemary, and add the lemon juice to the mixture. Stir well.
5. Arrange the bruschetta on a baking sheet and mound some of the zucchini on top of each one. Top with the cheese and warm in the oven just until the cheese melts.
6. Sprinkle with the mint, drizzle with olive oil, and serve.

(continued)

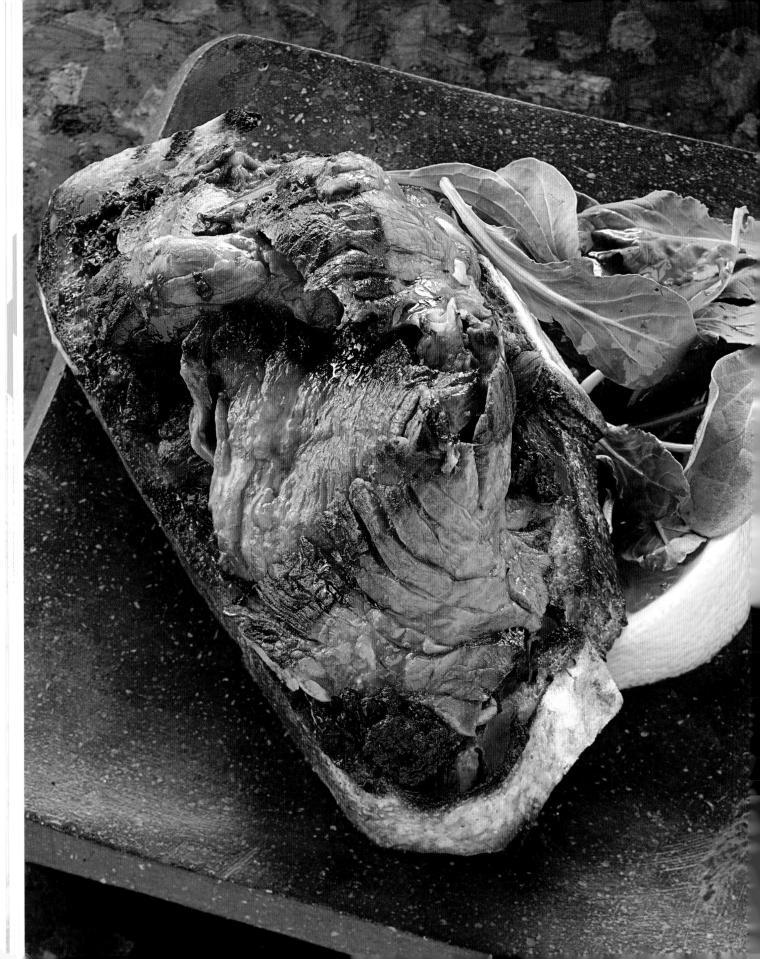

NOTE Fontina Val d'Aosta is classic fontina cheese from the region of Italy where this gorgeous cow's-milk cheese originated. All authentic Fontina Val d'Aosta is good and all is so labeled. Look, too, for the purple mountain peaks logo branded on every wheel of real Fontina Val d'Aosta to ascertain its origin. It's a lovely, mild cheese, easy to find, and good with many different foods and in many different ways, including melted, as here.

about the wine

The green flavors from the mint, rosemary, and zucchini are the most forward elements in this dish, with the fontina acting as a textural element. Choose your red wine carefully! To be avoided are significant oak, aggressive tannin, and unripe acidity. Find a fruity Barbera d'Asti from a producer like Coppo that will harmonize with the green.

While the flavors here are glorious, it's the color of the two lead ingredients that make it a super hit. Borlotti beans, also called cranberry beans, are red-speckled gems and when paired with the rosy prosciutto, the bruschetta is a smash! The beans top the bread and then are draped with a thin slice of prosciutto, which, as you have heard me say before, is the most luscious cured ham in the world. Try this. You'll love it.

bruschetta with borlotti beans
and prosciutto di parma | *serves 4*

1 1/4 cups dried borlotti or cranberry beans
1/2 pound bacon or pancetta, diced
1 cup chopped yellow onion
1 cup diced celery
1 cup diced fennel
1 1/2 teaspoons kosher salt
1 teaspoon cayenne
1/2 teaspoon freshly ground black pepper
2 teaspoons minced garlic
1 cup red wine
One 14 1/2-ounce can diced tomatoes
1 cup chicken stock, plus more if needed
2 tablespoons red wine vinegar
1 bay leaf
1 tablespoon unsalted butter
8 slices Rick's Basic Bruschetta (page 112)
1 tablespoon chopped fresh basil
1 teaspoon chopped fresh sage
8 thin slices prosciutto di Parma
Extra virgin olive oil

1. Put the beans in a bowl or pot and add enough cold water to cover. Set aside to soak at room temperature for at least 8 hours. Change the water once or twice, if possible.
2. Drain the beans, transfer to a heavy-bottomed pot, and add water to cover by an inch or two. Bring the water to a boil over high heat. Reduce the heat to medium-low, skim off any foam

The last time I went to the River Café in London, I didn't have much time, so I grabbed a seat at the bar and ordered just a few things to try. Okay, ten or twelve things! I was the only person at the bar and I remember how the waiter just glanced at me with that knowing look that said, "You must be a chef!" This is similar to one of those dishes, and as I ate it, gazing out over the Thames River, I was charmed. The caponata soaked into the bread while the raisins and pine nuts added sweet overlays of flavor. Serve this with an arugula salad for a very nice beginning dish.

Toma Maccagno is semisoft ripened cow's-milk cheese from Italy's Piedmont region. Its mild flavor, pale gold interior, bloomed rind, and round shape make it comparable to Camembert and Brie.

bruschetta with eggplant caponata | *serves 4*

About $1^1/4$ pounds eggplant
$^1/4$ cup olive oil
$^3/4$ cup chopped onion
$^1/3$ cup chopped celery
1 red bell pepper, cut into $^1/4$-inch dice
1 yellow bell pepper, cut into $^1/4$-inch dice
2 garlic cloves, minced
Juice of 1 orange
3 plum tomatoes, cut into $^1/4$-inch dice
$^1/3$ cup chopped pitted green olives
$^1/4$ cup red wine vinegar
3 tablespoons drained, chopped capers
$^1/4$ cup lightly toasted pine nuts
3 tablespoons golden raisins
1 to 2 tablespoons sugar
8 slices Rick's Basic Bruschetta (page 112)
1 cup grated Toma Maccagno cheese
2 tablespoons extra virgin olive oil
2 tablespoons chopped fresh flat-leaf parsley
Cracked black pepper

1. Without peeling the eggplant, cut it into $^1/_4$-inch dice. You should have $3^1/_2$ cups.
2. In a heavy skillet, heat 2 tablespoons of the oil over medium-high heat until hot but not smoking. Add the eggplant and cook, stirring, for 3 to 5 minutes, or until tender. Using a slotted spoon, transfer the eggplant to a bowl.
3. Add the remaining 2 tablespoons of oil to the skillet and cook the onion, celery, bell peppers, and garlic, stirring, for about 5 minutes, or until the onion softens. Add the orange juice and cook at a rapid simmer for about 2 minutes, or until reduced by half.
4. Add the tomatoes, olives, vinegar, capers, pine nuts, and raisins. Stir and then add the sugar, using a little more or less to taste. Cover the pan, reduce the heat to medium, and cook, stirring occasionally, for 5 to 10 minutes, until the mixture is thoroughly cooked and the celery is tender.
5. Transfer the vegetables to the bowl with the eggplant, mix the caponata gently, cover, let cool, then refrigerate for at least 6 hours and up to 12 hours.
6. Let the caponata come to room temperature and spoon a generous amount on top of each bruschetta. Garnish with the cheese, olive oil, parsley, and pepper, and serve.

about the wine

The sweet and sour that makes this bruschetta so delicious is also the element that makes the search for the appropriate wine a bit tricky. If you are in the mood for red wine, keep it simple. Those expensive tricks, which include fancy oak barrels, high extract, and high alcohols, will not help here. The simplest red will offer the most delights! Try the most inexpensive Nebbiolo you can find—not one that is aspiring to be Barbaresco or Barolo. Find one that is happy to be unclassified.

Its name is unfortunate, but when I first tasted lardo in Milan, I was convinced it was worth eating. When my good friend Chef Mario Batali cooked at Tru, he made an incredible spread using lardo, and it occurred to me that it would make a tasty bruschetta. I was right. The bread should be warm so that the thinly sliced lardo softens and melts a little into it for the ultimate bread-and-butter style of bruschetta. This is a very wine-friendly dish, as is true of bruschetta in general.

bruschetta with lardo and extra virgin olive oil | *serves 4*

2 tablespoons extra virgin olive oil
1 teaspoon chopped fresh oregano
$^1/2$ pound lardo (see Note)
8 slices Rick's Basic Bruschetta (page 112)
Kosher salt and cracked black pepper

1. In a small bowl, mix the olive oil and oregano. Set aside for 15 minutes to infuse the olive oil with the herb.
2. Slice the lardo paper-thin and lay a few slices on top of each bruschetta. Drizzle with the oil and season with salt and pepper. Serve.

NOTE Lardo is hog lard that is salted and often flavored with herbs or spices. The Italian version of fatback, it's considered a Tuscan delicacy. Once you taste it, you will know why. Look for it in Italian markets or order it from a reputable online source. Slice lardo very thin with a cheese slicer, mandoline, or potato peeler so that it melts in the mouth and provides just a hint of flavor and texture.

about the wine

While many red wines play nice with a dish of lardo bruschetta, we love it most on a cold, wintry Chicago night with a big bottle of Barolo. Who needs long underwear when these outrageously rich flavors are sure to keep you warm anywhere you try this combination? Some of our favorite classic-style Barolo producers are Giacomo Conterno, Mascarello, and Pio Cesare.

If you like hummus—and most people do—you will love this bean puree, which could be called an Italian version of the classic bean spread. For my mother, ceci beans (chickpeas) were a household staple, so they are for me, too. I keep cans in my pantry at all times because they are so versatile. You could cook your own instead of relying on canned, but for this puree I find the canned beans are just fine. And so much easier. Don't scrimp on the olive oil—you want the puree to be juicy and rich. The squeeze of lemon juice at the end will make you sing "hallelujah!"

bruschetta with spicy ceci bean puree | *serves 4*

2 garlic cloves

$^1/_2$ teaspoon kosher salt

One 16-ounce can ceci beans (also called chickpeas and garbanzo beans),
      drained and rinsed

$^1/_2$ cup tahini

$^1/_4$ cup finely chopped red onion

$^1/_4$ cup olive oil, plus more for drizzling

2 tablespoons fresh lemon juice

1 tablespoon balsamic vinegar

1 tablespoon crushed red pepper flakes (use more or less to taste)

$1^1/_2$ teaspoons honey

Kosher salt and freshly ground black pepper

8 slices Rick's Basic Bruschetta (page 112)

1 tablespoon roughly chopped, toasted pine nuts

1 tablespoon chopped fresh tarragon

1 tablespoons chopped fresh flat-leaf parsley

8 lemon wedges

1.   On a cutting board and using the blade and flat side of a large, sharp knife, mince and mash the garlic and salt to make a paste.

2.   In the bowl of a food processor fitted with the metal blade, pulse the ceci beans with the garlic paste, tahini, onion, the $^1/_4$ cup of oil, lemon juice, vinegar, red pepper, and honey. Scrape down the sides of the bowl several times and pulse until the mixture is smooth. Season to taste with salt and black pepper. The texture of the paste should be that of spreadable peanut butter; if necessary, thin it with water and pulse again.   *(continued)*

3. Spread the bean paste on the bruschetta. Sprinkle with pine nuts, tarragon, and parsley. Drizzle with olive oil, and serve garnished with lemon wedges for squeezing over the bruschetta.

about the wine

Old school is never a bad thing in our book. In Barbaresco, being old school means using Nebbiolo to produce classic, age-worthy wines in which the fruit, not the barrel used to age the juice, is the star. You'll need one with a bit of bottle age for this bruschetta. When we get a hankering for classic Barbaresco, we choose bottlings from Ceretto or Giacosa.

One Sunday after church, I made this bruschetta with skirt steak and my kids dubbed it the "ultimate Italian beef sandwich." This is a high compliment from three boys who live in Chicago, because Italian beef sandwiches are famous Chicago street food, and I am known to tout my love for these sandwiches (along with foie gras and caviar). I tend to agree with the boys about this bruschetta. Skirt steak is full of flavor, and when well marinated and carefully grilled, it's *fantastico*. Thanks to Gio, Brian, and Sean for recognizing a great sandwich!

bruschetta with skirt steak and tapenade | *serves 4*

$1^1/2$ cups olive oil
$^1/2$ cup balsamic vinegar
Juice of $^1/2$ lemon, plus 1 tablespoon
$^1/2$ cup chopped fresh flat-leaf parsley
$^1/4$ cup chopped fresh basil
3 tablespoons minced garlic
2 tablespoons minced shallots
1 tablespoon chopped fresh oregano
$^1/4$ teaspoon crushed red pepper flakes
Kosher salt and cracked black pepper
$1^1/2$ pounds skirt steak
Vegetable oil spray
2 cups arugula
1 to 2 tablespoons extra virgin olive oil, plus more for drizzling
$^1/4$ cup Tramonto's Tapenade (page 131)
8 slices Rick's Basic Bruschetta (page 112)
8 lemon wedges

1. In the bowl of a food processor fitted with the metal blade, combine the olive oil, vinegar, juice of $^1/2$ lemon, parsley, basil, garlic, shallots, and oregano. Pulse until well blended but not pureed. Add the red pepper and season to taste with salt and black pepper.
2. Lay the steak in a shallow nonreactive dish and pour the marinade over it. Cover with plastic wrap and refrigerate for at least 4 hours and up to 12 hours. Turn the steak in the marinade several times.

(continued)

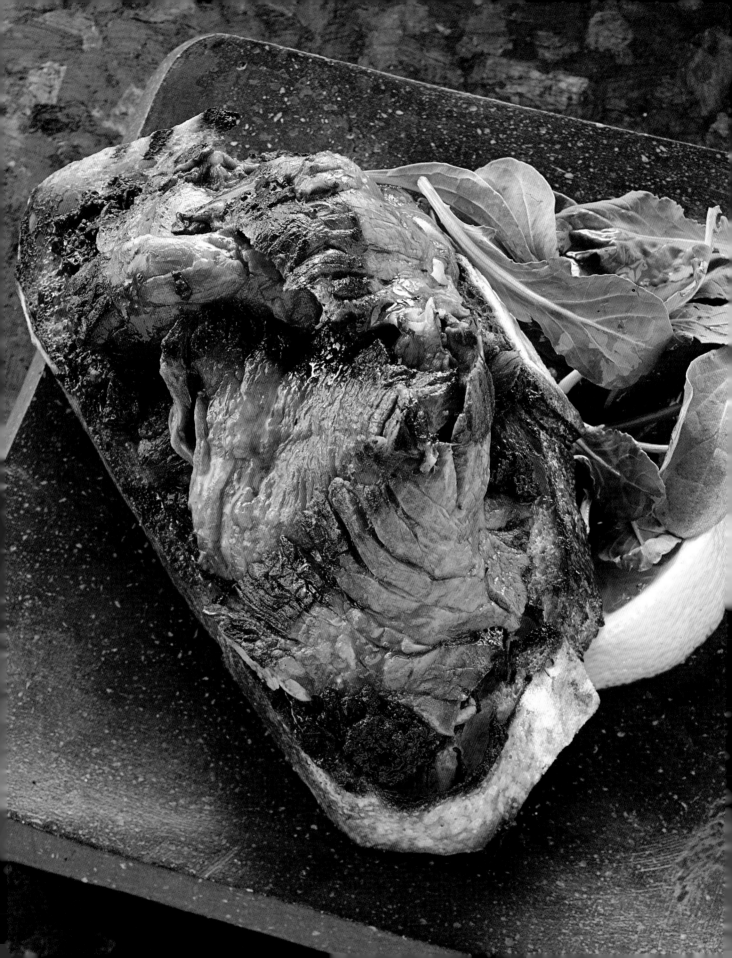

3. Prepare a charcoal or gas grill; the coals or heating elements should be medium hot. Lightly spray the grilling rack with vegetable oil spray to prevent sticking.

4. Lift the steak from the marinade and brush off the excess. Grill for 6 minutes, turn the steak, and grill for 6 to 8 minutes more for medium-rare. Transfer to a cutting board and let the steak rest for 5 to 7 minutes. Slice the steak across the grain into $1/2$-inch-wide strips.

5. In a mixing bowl, toss the arugula with a little olive oil (you may not need it all), the remaining tablespoon of lemon juice, and pinch of salt and pepper.

6. Spread some tapenade on each slice of bruschetta and top with slices of steak. Garnish each with the arugula salad. Drizzle with more olive oil and serve each bruschetta with a lemon wedge.

about the wine

The ultimate steak sandwich calls for one of Italy's ultimate reds. If there was any doubt about this dish's affinities, the balsamic, meaty skirt steak and olive tapenade kick it into big red wine territory. New-school producers like Sandrone and Fontanafredda of Barolo infuse their wines with flavors that are at once weighty and intense, but also accessible in their youth.

tramonto's tapenade | makes about 1$1/2$ cups

3 anchovy fillets
1 garlic clove, minced
1 tablespoon chopped fresh thyme
1 teaspoon grated orange zest
1 cup pitted Kalamata olives, plus more as needed
$1/4$ cup extra virgin olive oil, plus more as needed

1. In the bowl of a food processor fitted with the metal blade, process the anchovies, garlic, thyme, and zest until smooth.

2. Add the olives and olive oil and pulse until smooth. If the tapenade is thin, add more olives. If too thick, add a little more olive oil.

3. If not using immediately, transfer the tapenade to a nonreactive bowl, pour just enough olive oil over it to cover, and refrigerate for up to 1 week.

CHAPTER 6

crostini

little toasts with
refined toppings

Crostini
are to bruschetta what an opera is
to a rock concert. Each is spectacular in its own
right, but the former is more refined than the latter.
And, as with music, there is a time and place for both. My
basic crostini are made with small slices of bread cut from long,
slender baguettes, toasted, and flavored with garlic and butter. Yes, butter.
Not olive oil. You won't be surprised when I urge you to buy the best butter
you can find. Look for European-style butters, which are lower in moisture and
higher in flavor than most run-of-the-mill butters. (For more on these great butters,
see page 135.) I top these little toasts with gorgeous fillings, such as delicate crab
salad, figs and mascarpone cheese, and sun-dried tomatoes with fresh mozzarella. All
delicious, all appealing, but not as bold as the bruschetta toppings in the previous
chapter. These would be perfect to pass at a cocktail party. Make three or four and all
you need are the guests and the wine!

ABOUT THE WINE

*With crostini in your left hand, wrap the thumb and pointer finger of your right hand
around the stem of the sparkling wine flute. Bring the crostini to the mouth with your
left hand, and follow with a sip of one of Italy's delicious sparkling wines. In the
bubbly department, Italy has it all, from the sophisticated and refined
Franciacortas made in the méthode champenoise in Lombardy to
simple, sweet Brachetto from Piedmont. We love every one of
them, from the venerable Erbaluce di Caluso to the
simple Lambrusco and everything in
between!*

What is the difference between crostini and bruschetta? In general, crostini are more sophisticated and smaller. The bread slices for my crostini are about two inches across and thinner than those for bruschetta. When topped with great flavors, they fit the definition of a powerful tiny bite that by virtue of their size are less overwhelming than bruschetta. Crostini are always toasted, never grilled, and when you make them with the best, freshest bread available and sweet creamery butter, they become the ultimate garlic toasts. I pile everything on them under the Tuscan sun, even scrambled eggs at breakfast.

rick's basic crostini | *serves 4*

3 garlic cloves
Pinch of kosher salt
8 tablespoons (1 stick) high-quality salted butter, softened (see Note)
1 teaspoon fresh lemon juice
Cracked black pepper
Eight ^{1}/4-inch-thick slices baguette

1. On a cutting board, finely chop the garlic and sprinkle the salt over it. Keep chopping and smashing the garlic and salt together to make a paste. Use a wide-bladed knife so you can smear the paste along its flat side. You can also do this in a mortar and pestle.
2. In a small bowl, mix the butter, lemon juice, and garlic paste. Fold the softened butter over and onto the garlic mixture, mashing it down with the back of a spoon or spatula. Season to taste with pepper and continue folding.
3. Lay a sheet of plastic wrap on a work surface. Scrape the butter onto the plastic and use the plastic wrap to shape the butter into a log, encased in the plastic wrap. Refrigerate until ready to use. If not using within 3 days, you can freeze the garlic butter for up to 2 months. Let the butter soften before using.
4. Preheat the oven to 375°F.
5. Lay the bread on a baking sheet and brush both sides with garlic butter. Bake for 6 to 7 minutes, turning once, until golden brown but not too crispy. Let cool before using.

good butter

The difference between really good butter and all other butter lies with the butterfat content of the cream, which depends in large part on the cows and on how the cream is handled before it's churned into butter. The best butter from Europe is made from raw or cultured cream and, particularly that made from raw cream, might not be imported to the United States. But never fear: at American companies such as the Vermont Butter & Cheese Company, the butter is made from high-grade cream (a high butterfat content) that is cultured and then churned. The butter is rich and flavorful and when it's salted, its salt content is significantly lower than typical salted butter. This is what I use in my crostini recipes, so depending on the salted butter you choose, you may not need to add any salt. As with all ingredients for these recipes, choose the best butter you can. It pays off in terms of taste.

Don't look any further for a succulent crab salad open-face sandwich. The little garlic toasts piled high with rich, moist crab can be polished off in one or two bites. I can't think of a better way to start a meal! Don't skimp on the crabmeat. You need only a pound, so buy the best you can find. Bon appetit!

crostini with lump crab salad and
extra virgin olive oil | *serves 4 to 6*

1 pound fresh lump crabmeat
$^1/_2$ cup extra virgin olive oil, plus more for drizzling
1 roasted red bell pepper, seeded and diced (see Note, page 117)
1 tablespoon minced fresh chives
1 tablespoon torn fresh basil
Juice and grated zest of 1 lemon
Kosher salt and cracked black pepper
8 to 12 slices Rick's Basic Crostini (page 134)

1. Pick through the crabmeat to remove any bits of shell. Transfer to a nonreactive bowl.
2. Add the $^1/_2$ cup of olive oil, bell pepper, chives, basil, lemon juice, and zest and mix well. Season to taste with salt and pepper.
3. Top each crostini with about 1 tablespoon of the crab mixture. Drizzle with olive oil and serve.

about the wine

Ligurian winemaker Pierluigi Lugano of Bisson collaborates with a friend in the Veneto to produce a distinctive style of Prosecco, which is a natural match with the crab salad on this crostini. It is an early-bottled, atypically bone-dry style that almost reminds us of the Cinque Terre whites he produces, which smell like the Mediterranean Sea.

My wife, Eileen, loves egg salad and asparagus as much as I do and one day, when we had the components, I made these crostini. We carried them outside one beautiful spring afternoon to our backyard, where we like to spend time sitting by the pond, and we were both charmed by them. I decided they made lovely springtime crostini.

crostini with chopped egg and asparagus | *serves 4*

8 medium asparagus spears
4 large hard-cooked eggs, chopped
2 tablespoons diced red onion
1^1/2 teaspoons Dijon mustard
2 to 3 tablespoons Tarragon Mayonnaise (page 140)
8 slices Rick's Basic Crostini (page 134)
Extra virgin olive oil
Kosher salt and freshly ground black pepper

1. Bring a large saucepan of lightly salted water to a boil. Cook the asparagus for 5 to 7 minutes, or until tender. Drain and submerge in ice water. Drain again.
2. Diagonally cut the asparagus into ^{1}/4-inch slices. Reserve the tips for garnish. Transfer the slices to a nonreactive bowl.
3. Add the eggs, onion, and mustard. Stir in enough mayonnaise to bind and moisten the ingredients.
4. Spoon the egg-asparagus mixture on the crostini. Garnish with asparagus tips, drizzle with olive oil, and serve.

about the wine

Chefs love to parade the notoriously-difficult-to-pair-with-wine asparagus in their dishes in the springtime, so it is lucky that sommeliers have rosé sparkling wines with which to do battle. To the classic combination of eggs, tarragon, and asparagus, a crisp sparkling rosé with prominent Pinot Noir character will add a nice fruit element and avoid the dangers of turning metallic or tannic. We like the Franciacorta rosé from Bellavista, which is made from the classic varietals Chardonnay, Pinot Noir, and Pinot Bianco.

tarragon mayonnaise | makes about 1 ^{1}/4 cups

1 large egg
1 tablespoon fresh lemon juice
^{1}/2 cup olive oil
1 tablespoon chopped fresh tarragon
Pinch of cayenne
^{1}/2 cup canola oil
Kosher salt and freshly ground black pepper

1. In the bowl of a food processor fitted with the metal blade or in a blender, process the egg and lemon juice for 10 seconds. With the machine running, slowly pour in the olive oil until incorporated.
2. Add the tarragon and cayenne and then, with the machine running, slowly pour in the canola oil until emulsified. If the mayonnaise is too thick, thin it with 1 or 2 tablespoons of water. Season to taste with salt and pepper.

Anyone who has eaten at my fine-dining restaurants Trio and Tru knows that it's a passion of mine to deconstruct a classic recipe and then reconstruct it as a new dish. Thus, I took apart linguine with clam sauce to create this crostini. I've always favored dipping bread in the familiar pasta sauce over eating the actual dish, so I decided it would make a tasty crostini. And it does!

crostini with chopped clams and pancetta | *serves 4*

24 littleneck or Manila clams
2 tablespoons olive oil
Kosher salt and cracked black pepper
$^1/_2$ cup white wine
$^1/_2$ finely chopped onion
2 tablespoons chopped garlic
1 teaspoon crushed red pepper flakes
1$^1/_2$ teaspoons chopped fresh thyme
8 ounces pancetta, diced
$^1/_2$ cup seasoned panko (Japanese bread crumbs)
Juice of $^1/_2$ lemon
1 tablespoon chopped fresh flat-leaf parsley
1 tablespoon chopped fresh tarragon
1 tablespoon chopped fresh basil
8 slices Rick's Basic Crostini (page 134)
Extra virgin olive oil

1. To prepare the clams, gently scrub the shells with a soft brush. Transfer to a pot and cover with cold water. Set aside to soak for 1 hour. Change the water three times during the soaking to clean out any excess sand. Discard any clams that are cracked or partially open.

2. In a large sauté pan, heat the oil over medium-high heat. When the oil is hot, add the clams and season with salt and black pepper. Cover and cook for 6 to 8 minutes.

3. Add the wine, onion, garlic, red pepper, and thyme. Continue to sauté for 2 minutes longer or until the clam shells open completely. Discard any clams that do not open.

4. Remove the clams from the shells and roughly chop them. Discard the shells. Reserve the onion-garlic mixture in the pan.

(continued)

5. In a large skillet, cook the pancetta over medium heat until crispy. Drain off half of the fat and leave the rest in the pan with the pancetta. Add the clams and any liquid that has accumulated from them, as well as the reserved onion-garlic mixture.

6. Add the panko, lemon juice, parsley, tarragon, and basil and cook for 2 minutes, stirring, until well mixed. Do not let the mixture dry out; if necessary, add a little water.

7. Pile about 2 tablespoons of the clam mixture on each crostini. Drizzle with olive oil and serve.

about the wine

Single-vineyard Proseccos are a new addition to our wine cellar, and the "Crede" offering from Bisol in Valdobbiadene is a favorite. The Crede vineyard produces the fullest of Bisol's Proseccos while retaining the freshness that helps it counter the rich pancetta and the meaty clams.

I unabashedly love beef tartare and yes, this is my favorite crostini, particularly because I gild the lily with a drizzle of truffle oil! Steak tartare has been around for a good long time, and according to legend, its name refers to the Tartars, the nomads who roamed eastern Europe, for a time under the leadership of Attila the Hun. Fierce and bloodthirsty, the Tartars purportedly ate raw meat for strength. Tartars were Huns, but "beef hun" just doesn't have the panache of beef, or steak, tartare. If you've never had beef tartare, try it my way; then make it your way by omitting what you may not like such as capers, Worcestershire sauce, or anchovies. But don't fool with the beef. Buy the best you can from a reputable butcher. I use prime beef when possible, but because it is sometimes hard to find, I may turn to high-quality choice beef instead.

crostini with beef tartare and
white truffle oil | *serves 4*

2 anchovy fillets
2 garlic cloves, chopped
^{1}/2 cup minced shallots
1 tablespoon drained, chopped capers
1 large egg
2 tablespoons Dijon mustard
1^1/2 teaspoons grated orange zest
^{1}/4 cup olive oil
1 teaspoon Worcestershire sauce
1 pound beef tenderloin, freshly ground
Kosher salt and cracked black pepper
8 slices Rick's Basic Crostini (page 134)
^{1}/4 cup chopped fresh flat-leaf parsley
1 tablespoon white truffle oil

1. In a chilled mixing bowl, mash the anchovies and garlic with a fork to make a paste. Add the shallots and capers and mash them into the paste. Add the egg and whisk it into the paste with the fork. Whisk in the mustard and orange zest.
2. In a slow, steady stream, add the olive oil, whisking constantly until incorporated. Whisk in the Worcestershire sauce.

(continued)

3. Add the beef and mix well with a wooden spoon. Season to taste with salt and pepper.
4. Mound some tartare in the center of each crostini. Garnish with parsley and drizzle with truffle oil.

about the wine

With all of the high-toned elements in this dish, like capers, mustard, and Worcestershire, it is important that the accompanying wine not be flabby. This need for acid, and the Piedmontese element of white truffle in the dish, directs us to the zingy, white, sparkling Erbaluce di Caluso from the same region. This varietal is ideal for sparkling wine production because of its tendency to high acidity. When produced by a deft winery like Luigi Ferrando, the result is one of Italy's cult wines: "Cariola."

When I lived on East Tenth Street in New York's Greenwich Village back in the 1980s, Il Cantinori was our neighborhood restaurant, and I ate there often. I always liked the restaurant's little starters, in particular a sausage-topped crostini that has been part of my taste memory for years. I have since created my own. It's a perfect one-biter with all the right elements: rich, meaty sausage tossed with sautéed spinach, lemon juice, and olive oil. I like spicy Italian sausage but you could substitute any sausage.

crostini with spicy italian sausage and spinach | *serves 4*

1 pound large-leaf spinach, thick stems removed
Juice of $^1/_2$ lemon
1 tablespoon olive oil
Kosher salt and cracked black pepper
1 pound spicy Italian sausage, crumbled
2 garlic cloves, thinly sliced
8 slices Rick's Basic Crostini (page 134)
8 large shavings pecorino cheese (about 2 tablespoons)

1. Bring a large pot of lightly salted water to a boil. Cook the spinach for 1 to 2 minutes, until wilted and tender. Drain. When cool enough, using your hands or a dish towel, squeeze as much excess water as possible from the spinach. Chop the spinach and transfer to a bowl. Add the lemon juice and olive oil, and season to taste with salt and pepper. Set aside.

2. In a large sauté pan, sauté the sausage over medium heat until cooked through. With a slotted spoon remove the sausage and set it aside. Reserve the rendered fat.

3. Heat the fat over medium heat. Add the garlic and cook just until lightly browned. Take care not to burn the garlic.

4. Return the sausage to the pan and add the spinach. Toss until heated through, then season to taste with salt and pepper.

5. Pile some sausage onto each crostini and garnish with shavings of pecorino.

about the wine

A dry, slightly sparkling Lambrusco is ideal. These Lambrusco have all of the fruit and none of the sweetness of the other kind. Try "Terre Calda" dry Lambrusco from Ca' de Medici in Emilia-Romagna. Make your friends close their eyes before they taste if you have to.

This crostini is about the sweet caramelized onions that, when layered on the little garlic toasts, make me think of the crusty topping on French onion soup. The saltiness of the prosciutto livens up the crostini, making it just about perfect for a crisp fall day.

crostini with prosciutto di parma and caramelized onions | *serves 4*

1 tablespoon unsalted butter
$^1/_3$ cup olive oil
1 cup thinly sliced Vidalia or other sweet onion
1 tablespoon sugar
2 garlic cloves, minced
$^1/_2$ tablespoon chopped fresh thyme
8 thin slices Prosciutto di Parma
8 slices Rick's Basic Crostini (page 134)
Kosher salt and freshly cracked black pepper
1 tablespoon chopped flat-leaf parsley

1. In a sauté pan, melt the butter over medium heat. Add the olive oil and the onions. Sprinkle with the sugar and sauté the onions for 5 to 6 minutes, or until evenly caramelized and golden brown. Before the onions are cooked, add the garlic and thyme and cook, stirring, until the garlic browns lightly. Season to taste with salt and pepper.

2. Lay a slice of prosciutto on each of the crostini and top each with the onion mixture. Drizzle with any juice left over in the pan, garnish with parsley, and serve.

In one little bite, your mouth fills with the earthy, intoxicating flavors of three different kinds of wild mushrooms. Not too many of these are actually foraged from the woods, because nowadays, many of the mushrooms that used to be considered wild are actually cultivated. However, that does not make them any less delectable. Try this with the mushrooms I list here, or substitute any you see in the market. The mushrooms are splendid spooned onto crostini, but you could also toss them with pasta. They are great little bites to serve to friends when you're standing around in the kitchen drinking wine. All great parties end up in the kitchen anyway, so why not just start there?

crostini with wild mushroom ragu | *serves 4*

$^1/_2$ cup olive oil

2 garlic cloves, minced

1 tablespoon minced shallot

1 cup sliced cremini mushrooms

1 cup quartered chanterelle mushrooms

1 cup quartered oyster mushrooms

$^1/_3$ cup white wine

1 cup chicken stock

$^1/_2$ cup heavy cream

Grated zest of $^1/_2$ orange

1 tablespoon unsalted butter

1$^1/_2$ teaspoons chopped fresh thyme

1 cup peeled, seeded, and diced plum tomatoes

2 tablespoons torn fresh basil

Extra virgin olive oil

Kosher salt and freshly ground black pepper

8 slices Rick's Basic Crostini (page 134)

1$^1/_2$ to 2 ounces Parmigiano-Reggiano cheese, shaved

1. In a sauté pan, heat the olive oil over medium heat. Add the garlic and shallot and cook for about 1 minute, until they begin to soften but do not color. Add the mushrooms and cook for 3 to 4 minutes, or until they soften and begin to release their moisture.

2. Add the wine and stir with a wooden spoon to deglaze the pan. Cook until the liquid thickens and reduces to a glaze. Add the chicken stock and cook for 6 to 8 minutes, or until reduced by half. Add the cream and bring to a boil over medium-high heat; then reduce the

heat to medium and simmer for about 2 minutes, or until reduced by half. Stir in the zest, butter, and thyme.

3. Meanwhile, in a small bowl, mix the tomato and basil. Add a drizzle of olive oil, toss, and season to taste with salt and pepper.

4. Spoon the mushroom mixture on top of the crostini. Garnish each plate with some tomatoes and cheese.

about the wine

Tenuta Cocci Griffoni makes a really interesting sparkling white wine called "Offida Passerina" in the central Italian wine region of Le Marche. It is a wildly perfumed, bright sparkler that adds an aromatic component to this crostini topping. Experiment with this one, though. Wild mushrooms are about as wine-friendly a component as exists in cuisine.

There's a reason figs have been treasured since ancient times: They are absolutely delicious. While there are numerous varieties, I make these crostini with small, sweet Black Mission figs, which are in season only for a short time in the spring and then for a slightly longer time in September. Team them with creamy, incredibly rich mascarpone cheese spiked with orange zest and you have crostini worthy of a poem. Figs must be eaten within a day or two of purchase, so you will have to make this when the figs appear in the markets, rather than when you feel the urge. Listen for the rhythms of the season as you walk through the markets.

crostini with grilled black mission figs and orange mascarpone | *serves 4*

FIGS
Vegetable oil spray
4 Black Mission figs
1 tablespoon olive oil
Kosher salt and freshly ground black pepper
2 teaspoons sugar

CROSTINI
About $^1/_2$ cup baby arugula (3 to 4 leaves per crostini)
2 tablespoons extra virgin olive oil, plus more for drizzling
Juice of $^1/_2$ lemon
1 tablespoon chopped fresh basil
Kosher salt and freshly ground black pepper
3 tablespoons mascarpone cheese
1 tablespoon heavy cream
1 teaspoon sugar
Grated zest of $^1/_2$ orange
8 slices Rick's Basic Crostini (page 134)

1. *For the figs:* Prepare a charcoal or gas grill or preheat a countertop grill. The coals or heating elements should be medium hot. Lightly spray the grilling rack with vegetable oil spray to prevent sticking. Alternatively, have a small blowtorch at the ready. *(continued)*

2. Slice the figs in half lengthwise and rub the cut sides with the olive oil. Sprinkle with salt and pepper.

3. Spread the sugar in a small plate. Dip the cut sides of the figs in the sugar to coat lightly. Grill the figs, sugared-side down, for 1 to 2 minutes, until caramelized. Set aside to rest for 2 minutes. If you use the blowtorch, run it over the sugared sides of the figs to caramelize.

4. *For the crostini:* In a bowl, toss the arugula with the olive oil, lemon juice, and basil. Season to taste with salt and pepper.

5. In another bowl, mix the mascarpone with the cream, sugar, and orange zest and whisk until creamy. Season to taste with salt and pepper.

6. Spread the mascarpone on the crostini. Top with a few arugula leaves and then a fig half, caramelized side up. Drizzle with olive oil and serve.

about the wine

Typical mass-produced Prosecco would be too simple and angular for the rich textures of the fig and mascarpone on this crostini. The acidity of Prosecco is necessary here though, so choose instead "garagiste" Prosecco producer Bele Casel, where they release their wines in tiny batches to ensure freshness. They are also known for extending the lees contact period, and the result is one of the creamiest Proseccos that we have ever tried. Mission fig + orange mascarpone + Bele Casel Prosecco = happiness.

This crostini makes perfect sense to me because my many aunts liked to pair chicken livers with balsamic vinegar. To this day, I believe it was the sweetness of the balsamic that made the livers palatable to a kid. When I grew up, I didn't think anything of putting the two together, so it's not surprising that I served this crostini when I opened Trio in 1993. It's been one of my standard bearers ever since. The lush fattiness of the livers offset by the sweet acid in the vinegar is stunning.

crostini with chicken livers and balsamic | *serves 4*

$1/2$ pound chicken livers, trimmed
Whole milk, enough to cover livers
$1/4$ cup extra virgin olive oil, plus more for drizzling
3 anchovy fillets, rinsed, patted dry, and chopped
$1/2$ cup minced onion
1 garlic clove, minced
$1/3$ cup aged balsamic vinegar
$1^1/2$ teaspoons chopped fresh sage
Kosher salt and cracked black pepper
1 tablespoon unsalted butter, softened
8 slices Rick's Basic Crostini (page 134)
2 tablespoons drained, chopped capers
1 tablespoon chopped fresh flat-leaf parsley

1. Rinse the livers in cold water and pat dry with paper towels. Transfer to a bowl and add enough milk to cover completely. Refrigerate for at least 4 hours and up to 6 hours. Drain the livers, rinse lightly in cold water, and pat dry.

2. In a medium skillet, heat the $1/4$ cup of olive oil over medium heat, and sauté the anchovies for about 2 minutes. Add the onion and sauté for 3 to 4 minutes, until softened and lightly browned. Add the garlic and sauté for about 2 minutes, until softened but not colored.

3. Add the chicken livers and cook for 4 to 5 minutes, or until lightly browned. Add the vinegar and sage, season to taste with salt and pepper, and sauté for 2 to 3 minutes longer, until the flavors blend.

4. Transfer the contents of the skillet to the bowl of a food processor fitted with a metal blade and pulse to a chunky puree.

5. Transfer the puree to a nonreactive bowl, whisk in the butter, and season to taste with salt and pepper.
6. Spread each crostini with about 2 tablespoons of the liver. Garnish each with capers, parsley, and a drizzle of olive oil.

about the wine

Though oft maligned, fruity Lambrusco is one of our favorite food wines. Emilia-Romagna is the home of both balsamic vinegar from Modena and the viticulture region that produces these sometimes *frizzante* reds, which are chock-full of blueberry and blackberry flavors. The vinegar in the dish helps take the edge off the chicken livers, and the acidity of the Lambrusco takes you the rest of the way.

Many people are fearful of salt cod, which is too bad because it's so delicious. Hands down, the best I ever tasted was in New York at my friend Chef Eric Ripert's restaurant, Le Bernardin, which inspired me to go home and work on mine. Making this fish spread is time-consuming, I admit, but only because you have to plan well ahead of time. The actual cooking and mixing are simple and once you make a batch, you'll be convinced to try it again and again. I serve it alongside grilled fish instead of mashed potatoes, stir it into scrambled eggs, and eat it with salads. It's way more flavorful than mashed potatoes and wow! On a crostini . . . it's amazing!

crostini baccala | *serves 4*

1 pound salt cod (see Note)
3^1/2 cups whole milk
^{1}/2 teaspoon crushed red pepper flakes
1 bay leaf
1 sprig fresh thyme
7 garlic cloves
^{1}/2 onion, diced
Kosher salt and cracked black pepper
^{1}/2 pound Yukon Gold potatoes, peeled and diced
^{1}/4 cup heavy cream
2 tablespoons olive oil
1 tablespoon fresh lemon juice
1 tablespoon chopped fresh chives
8 slices Rick's Basic Crostini (page 134)
Grated lemon zest
1 tablespoon chopped fresh flat-leaf parsley

1. In a shallow pan, cover the cod with cold water and refrigerate for 24 hours. Change the water every 8 hours and take care to keep the fish as intact as possible.
2. In a large saucepan, combine the milk, red pepper, bay leaf, and thyme. Crush 5 of the garlic cloves and add them to the pan with the onion, season to taste with salt and pepper. Heat for about 5 minutes but do not let the milk boil.
3. Put the cod in the hot milk and poach at a gentle simmer for 5 to 7 minutes, until the cod is tender. Using a slotted spoon, lift the cod from the pan and reserve the poaching liquid. When

cool enough to handle, remove the skin and any bones. Transfer the fish to the bowl of an electric mixer. Mince the remaining 2 cloves of garlic and add to the bowl.

4. Strain the poaching liquid and return it to the pan. Bring to a simmer over medium heat, add the potatoes, and cook for 15 to 20 minutes, until tender. Drain the potatoes and reserve the cooking liquid. Put the potatoes in the bowl with the cod.

5. With the mixer on medium speed, start blending the fish and potatoes. Add the heavy cream and then as much of the reserved poaching liquid as needed to give the consistency of mashed potatoes. With the mixer running, add the olive oil and lemon juice.

6. Reduce the speed to low and beat in the chives. Season to taste with salt and pepper.

7. Spread 1 or 2 tablespoons of the fish mixture on each crostini. Garnish with lemon zest and parsley.

NOTE If you cannot find salt cod, substitute fresh cod. Salt the fish generously with kosher salt, lay in a perforated pan or a colander set inside a larger pan, and refrigerate for 24 hours. There is no need to soak fresh cod, but rinse it well to remove all salt. If it looks like it might be too salty, soak it for about 10 minutes. Proceed with the recipe from step 2.

about the wine

Garlic-flavored, creamy salt cod crostini need a sparkling wine with toasty, leesy richness. The venerable Franciacorta is the answer here, and a prestige cuvée with a little bottle age is the way to take the match to the next level. Ca' del Bosco is one of our favorite producers in Lombardy, and makes tasty vintage Franciacorta. For a real treat, hunt down a bottle of Ca' del Bosco "Cuvée Annamaria Clementi." This wine is only made in great vintages and competes with the best that Champagne has to offer.

CHAPTER 7

panini

grilled sandwiches

When
I get home from work or on my days
off, I prefer to make sandwiches. After spending
the day cooking lightly seared fish, rich ragouts, foie gras,
and truffles, I crave something that gets right to the point with no
frills. Panini are all the rage, which, as a sandwich lover from way back,
awakens my inner Homer Simpson with a huge grin! Anything goes, and as
long as the bread is good, you can have a big, messy feast or a refined, tantalizing
light meal that hits the spot anytime, day or night. Panini are Italy's contribution to the
wide world of sandwiches, and as with all things Italian, are just a little better than other
grilled sandwiches. Why? I think it's the bread, the fillings, and the attitude. They may be
casual fare, but that does not mean they are carelessly conceived.
I like to use a panini maker for these grilled sandwiches because it applies pressure to both sides of
the bread at the same time for even heating, melting, crisping, softening, and oozing. But, even
though these small appliances (that somewhat resemble waffle irons) are not expensive, you may
rebel at the idea of yet *another* machine in your kitchen. I understand this. Just be sure to brown the
sandwich on both sides in a good pan until lightly browned. Don't rush it. It's worth it. Imagine
biting into a sandwich filled with grilled mushrooms and herby goat cheese, or one with Robiola
cheese melting on top of honey-kissed ham, offset with a sharp mustard mayo. Or how about the
ultimate grilled cheese panini made with over-the-top fontina and Gouda? You get the idea.

ABOUT THE WINE

*All we want with our panini is a glass of southern Italian goodness. Puglia, Calabria,
Basilicata, Sicily, and Sardegna bring on the big, rich, sandwich-friendly reds.
Explore spicy Puglian Primitivo, the brawny Gaglioppo and Aglianico of
Calabria and Basilicata, and the crowd-pleasing Nero d'Avola and
Monica di Sardegna of the islands. Step aside, grilled cheese
with tomato soup; we've found a new and very tasty
way to stay warm!*

It's just cheese on toast, but man, is it good! I combine two highly regarded and much-loved European cheeses: Fontina, because it's luscious and a little stringy when melted, and Gouda, because of its deeper foundation and richer texture. Gouda, you ask? Rather than the familiar red-rinded, semisoft cheese most of us know, I urge you to seek out aged Gouda, which is firmer, saltier, and grainier. It makes all the difference.

fontina, gouda, and tomato panini | *serves 4*

Eight ^{1}/4-inch-thick slices beefsteak tomato
Extra virgin olive oil
Kosher salt and freshly ground black pepper
4 tablespoons (1 stick) salted butter, softened, for brushing
Eight ^{1}/2-inch-thick slices ciabatta or Italian country-style bread
6 ounces smoked Gouda, cut into 4 slices
8 large basil leaves, stemmed
6 ounces Fontina, shredded, or more if desired
1 to 2 teaspoons olive oil

1. Lay the tomato slices on a plate and drizzle with extra virgin olive oil. Season to taste with salt and pepper and set aside for about 10 minutes to marinate at room temperature.
2. Using a pastry brush, lightly butter both sides of the bread. Set 4 slices aside.
3. Top each of the 4 slices with a slice of Gouda, 2 slices of tomato, and 2 basil leaves. Sprinkle with fontina. Top with the remaining 4 slices of bread.
4. Heat the olive oil in a small skillet over medium-high heat or brush a panini press with olive oil and preheat to high. Grill each sandwich in the skillet for 2 to 3 minutes on each side, until the bread is golden brown and the cheese melts. Press the sandwich with a spatula when you turn it over. If you use a panini press, grill the sandwiches for about 8 minutes, or until the bread is golden brown and the cheese melts.
5. Cut each sandwich into rectangles and slice the rectangles into bricks, or bars, each about 1 inch long. Stack on plates for serving.

about the wine

Primitivo is California Zinfandel's ancestor, and we love this big red in its old-school incarnation. The Italian wines tend to be more subtle and elegant than the New World versions, and that is exactly what makes Primitivo a great partner for this Italian grilled cheese and tomato sandwich.

This may be the ultimate grilled cheese sandwich. It's nothing more than three kinds of meltable cheese stacked on buttered bread and then grilled in a pan or panini press. The result? Sublime with every bite. The key is to buy the best fresh mozzarella, provolone, and Fontina cheese you can find so that they melt into each other for a perfect harmony of cheese and bread.

three-cheese panini | *serves 4*

4 tablespoons unsalted butter
Eight $^1/2$-inch-thick slices ciabatta or Italian country-style bread
4 ounces fresh mozzarella cheese, cut into 4 slices
6 ounces provolone cheese, cut into 4 slices
4 ounces Fontina cheese, cut into 4 slices
Kosher salt and freshly ground black pepper
About 1 teaspoon olive oil

1. Using a pastry brush, lightly butter both sides of the bread with butter. Set 4 slices aside.
2. Top each of the 4 slices with a slice of mozzarella, a slice of provolone, and slice of Fontina. Season lightly to taste with salt and pepper. Top with the remaining 4 slices of bread.
3. Heat the olive oil in a small skillet over medium-high heat or brush a panini press with olive oil and preheat to high. Grill each sandwich in the skillet for 2 to 3 minutes on each side, or until golden brown and the cheese melts. When one side of the sandwich is golden brown, turn it over and press the sandwich with a spatula. If you use a panini press, grill the sandwiches for about 8 minutes, or until the bread is golden brown and the cheese melts.
4. Cut the sandwich into rectangles and slice the rectangles into bricks, or bars, each about 1 inch long. Stack on plates for serving.

PLT stands for pancetta, lettuce, and tomato, and if you knew me, you would know that I am a BLT fanatic. When I travel, I always order BLTs or club sandwiches. Whether I am dining at a greasy spoon or a great hotel, stopping for lunch between meetings, or vacationing with my wife and kids, I am always on the hunt for the best—and have occasionally found the worst! Because the recipes in this book are inspired by Italian food, when I first made this sandwich with rich, salty pancetta and spread the bread with garlic aioli in place of mayo, I was very, very happy. When I grilled the sandwich and lifted it from the panini press, warm and soft with the aioli flavoring it through and through, you probably could see my grin all the way down Michigan Avenue!

plt | *serves 4*

8 thin slices pancetta (about $^1/_2$ pound)
4 tablespoons ($^1/_2$ stick) salted butter, softened, for brushing
Eight $^1/_2$-inch-thick slices ciabatta or Italian country-style bread
$^1/_4$ cup Roasted Garlic Aioli (page 161)
3 ripe plum tomatoes, sliced
4 inner leaves romaine lettuce
Kosher salt and freshly ground black pepper
1 to 2 teaspoons olive oil

1. In a skillet over medium heat, cook the pancetta until crisp. Drain on paper towels and set aside.
2. Using a pastry brush, lightly butter both sides of the bread. Set 4 slices aside.
3. Top each of the 4 slices with 1 tablespoon of aioli, 2 slices of pancetta, tomato slices, and a lettuce leaf. Season with salt and pepper. Top with the remaining 4 slices of bread.
4. Heat the olive oil in a small skillet over medium-high heat or brush a panini press with olive oil and preheat to high. Grill each sandwich in the skillet for 2 to 3 minutes on each side, until the bread is golden brown and the cheese melts. Press the sandwich with a spatula when you turn it over. If you use a panini press, grill the sandwiches for about 8 minutes, or until the bread is golden brown and the cheese melts.
5. Cut each sandwich into rectangles and slice the rectangles into bricks, or bars, each about 1 inch long. Stack on plates for serving.

Puglia specializes in deeply colored, rich reds, and those made from the Negroamaro grape are no exception. The roasted garlic aioli takes this bacon sandwich into the higher reaches of decadence, so a similarly full-throttle wine will do. Taurino "Notarpanaro" and Leone de Castris "Donna Lisa" are two Negroamaro-based wines from southern Italy that we can't stop drinking.

roasted garlic aioli | makes about 1 cup

1 garlic head (about 12 cloves)
$1^1/2$ teaspoons olive oil
Kosher salt
1 cup good-quality, store-bought mayonnaise
1 teaspoon fresh lemon juice
Cracked black pepper

1. Preheat the oven to 350°F.
2. Remove the outer layers of skin from the garlic head but leave the cloves intact at the root end. Put the head in the center of a sheet of aluminum foil, drizzle with the olive oil, and add a pinch of salt. Fold the foil over the top of the garlic to make a loose package. Put on a baking sheet and roast for 30 to 40 minutes, until the garlic is soft. Unwrap and set aside to cool.
3. When cool, squeeze the softened garlic pulp from each clove. Transfer the pulp to the bowl of a food processor fitted with the metal blade. Add the mayonnaise and lemon juice. Process until smooth. Season to taste with salt and pepper. Use immediately or cover and refrigerate for up to 3 days.

One of the most interesting little bites I had was with some friends in Venice at an *enoteca* where we stopped for a glass of wine. Instead of olives or nuts at the bar, the chef offered small, thin rectangles of bread spread with bright green pistachio pesto. The pesto alone was enough for the little slices of bread, but I thought it would be awesome as part of a sandwich, and jotted the idea in my notebook. Here is the result. *Fantastico!*

fresh mozzarella, roasted red peppers, and pistachio pesto panini | *serves 4*

4 tablespoons (^{1}/2 stick) salted butter, softened, for brushing
Eight ^{1}/2-inch-thick slices ciabatta or Italian country-style bread
1 cup Pistachio Pesto (page 163)
^{1}/2 pound fresh mozzarella cheese, drained and thinly sliced
2 roasted red bell peppers, halved (see Note, page 117)
Kosher salt and cracked black pepper
1 to 2 teaspoons olive oil

1. Using a pastry brush, lightly butter both sides of the bread. Set 4 slices aside.
2. Top each of the 4 slices with equal amounts of pesto and cheese and a pepper half. Season to taste with salt and pepper. Top with the remaining 4 slices of bread.
3. Heat the olive oil in a small skillet over medium-high heat or brush a panini press with olive oil and preheat to high. Grill each sandwich in the skillet for 2 to 3 minutes on each side, until the bread is golden brown and the cheese melts. Press the sandwich with a spatula when you turn it over. If you use a panini press, grill the sandwiches for about 8 minutes, or until the bread is golden brown and the cheese melts.
4. Cut each sandwich into rectangles and slice the rectangles into bricks, or bars, each about 1 inch long. Stack on plates for serving.

about the wine

Although green and red match beautifully at Christmastime, the two can cause issues for the palate when pistachio pesto is the green and a glass of juicy southern Italian wine is the red. Thankfully, the Sicilians are making many tasty whites that help you avoid the clash. One we like is the "Angimbe" blend from the Cusumano winery. It is an oaked blend of the aromatic Insolia grape and our old friend Chardonnay, which wakes up with the nutty pesto and has a nice texture that matches that of the fresh mozzarella.

pistachio pesto | makes about 1^1/2 cups

^{3}/4 cup ground pistachios (about 7 ounces nut meats)
^{1}/3 cup freshly grated Parmigiano-Reggiano cheese
1 cup packed fresh basil leaves
^{1}/3 cup extra virgin olive oil
1 teaspoon grated lemon zest
1 garlic clove
Cracked black pepper
^{1}/2 cup packed fresh flat-leaf parsley leaves, optional

1. In the bowl of a food processor fitted with a metal blade, combine the pistachios, cheese, basil, olive oil, lemon zest, and garlic. Process until smooth. Season to taste with pepper and pulse until mixed.
2. Add the parsley, if desired, and process until smooth. The parsley will help the pesto retain its color.
3. Transfer to a lidded glass or rigid plastic container. Cover tightly and refrigerate for up to 3 days. If you plan to store the pesto for longer than 24 hours, pour a film of olive oil over it.

When I was a child, it seemed that my mother or grandmother fried eggplant at least every other day, so our house always smelled delicious. To this day, the aroma and taste of fried eggplant take me back to Rochester, New York, and the house where I grew up. In those days, I slapped a piece of fried eggplant and tomato sauce on a slice of bread and ate it on the run. More often than not, my partner in crime was my best friend, Vinnie Rubert, who was a fried eggplant enthusiast, even at age ten. I was an only child and Vinnie came from a family of seven boys and one girl, so we appreciated what the other had. We also shared common food cultures, and both of us were always catching it for snatching food from whatever pan was on the stove when our mothers turned their backs.

fried eggplant, caramelized onion, and provolone panini | *serves 4*

1 cup all-purpose flour

2 large eggs, beaten

1 cup fresh or dried bread crumbs

1 pound eggplant, cut into $^1/4$-inch-thick rounds

$^1/4$ cup extra virgin olive oil

5 tablespoons unsalted butter

Kosher salt and cracked black pepper

1 pound yellow onions, very thinly sliced

1 teaspoon chopped fresh thyme

4 tablespoons ($^1/2$ stick) salted butter, softened, for brushing

Eight $^1/2$-inch-thick slices ciabatta or Italian country-style bread

$^1/2$ cup Tomato Sauce (page 167)

8 slices provolone cheese (about $^1/2$ pound)

1 to 2 teaspoons olive oil

1. Put the flour in one shallow dish, the beaten eggs in another, and the bread crumbs in a third. Dip the eggplant slices in the flour and tap off any excess. Next dip them in the egg and then the bread crumbs until coated on both sides. As each slice is coated, set it on a paper-towel–lined platter.

2. In a large sauté pan, heat the olive oil over medium-high heat until hot and shimmering. Add 1 tablespoon of unsalted butter and let it melt and foam. When the foam subsides, cook the

eggplant slices, turning once, for 2 to 3 minutes on each side, or until uniformly dark, golden brown. Drain on the paper-towel–lined platter and season with salt and pepper while hot.

3. In the same or another large skillet, melt the remaining 4 tablespoons of unsalted butter over medium-high heat. Add the onions, lower the heat to medium-low, and cook slowly, stirring occasionally, for 45 to 60 minutes, until golden brown and caramelized. Adjust the heat as needed to maintain slow, gentle cooking. Add the thyme and season to taste with salt. Remove the skillet from the heat and cover to keep warm.

4. Using a pastry brush, lightly butter both sides of the bread with the salted butter. Set 4 slices aside.

5. Top each of the 4 slices with 3 or 4 slices of eggplant, about 2 tablespoons of onions, 2 tablespoons of tomato sauce, and 1 slice of cheese. Top with the remaining 4 slices of bread.

6. Heat the olive oil in a small skillet over medium-high heat or brush a panini press with olive oil and preheat to high. Grill each sandwich in the skillet for 2 to 3 minutes on each side, until the bread is golden brown and the cheese melts. Press the sandwich with a spatula when you turn it over. If you use a panini press, grill the sandwiches for about 8 minutes, or until the bread is golden brown and the cheese melts.

7. Cut each sandwich into rectangles and slice the rectangles into bricks, or bars, each about 1 inch long. Stack on plates for serving.

about the wine

Monica di Sardegna is an eponymously named wine. It's tasty, bright cherry red, and perfect to enjoy with the dense fried eggplant, sweet caramelized onions, and melted provolone. Cantina Santadi is a top-flight co-op on the island of Sardegna that produces an excellent example of this wine.

tomato sauce | makes about 2^1/2 cups

2 tablespoons olive oil
^{1}/2 cup diced yellow onion
3 garlic cloves, minced
1 tablespoon tomato paste
One 28-ounce can crushed tomatoes, with juice, or 2 pounds
     fresh plum tomatoes, peeled, seeded, and diced
1 cup chicken stock
3 tablespoons unsalted butter
3 tablespoons torn fresh basil
Kosher salt and cracked black pepper

1. In a medium saucepan, heat the olive oil over medium heat and sauté the onion for about 5 minutes, until softened. Add the garlic and cook for about 1 minute longer, until softened but not colored. Stir in the tomato paste and tomatoes and cook for about 3 minutes.
2. Add the stock and bring to a boil over medium-high heat. Reduce the heat to medium and simmer for about 20 minutes or until the sauce thickens.
3. Whisk in the butter, a piece at a time; wait until the butter is incorporated before adding the next piece. Stir in the basil and season to taste with salt and pepper. Use immediately or cool, cover, and refrigerate for up to 3 days or freeze for up to 1 month.

I ate at my friend Chef Nancy Silverton's Los Angeles restaurant, Pizzeria Mozza, several years ago. I chowed down on Nancy's out-of-control panini, and thought she had hit on an awesome sandwich. This is hardly surprising. Nancy is a breakthrough chef, and her sandwiches and panini are as good as they get. Naturally I had to go home and come up with my own over-the-top rendition! Thanks, Nancy!

grilled portobello mushrooms with herb goat cheese panini | *serves 4*

4 medium to large portobello mushrooms
$^1/_2$ cup olive oil, plus more for oiling the pan
$^1/_4$ cup aged balsamic vinegar
2 garlic cloves, minced
Kosher salt and cracked black pepper
Vegetable oil spray
4 tablespoons ($^1/_2$ stick) salted butter, softened, for brushing
Eight $^1/_2$-inch-thick slices ciabatta or Italian country-style bread
$^1/_2$ cup Goat Cheese Spread (page 169)
White truffle oil, optional

1. Using a soft brush, remove any excess dirt from the mushrooms and then use a spoon to scoop out the gills. Put the mushrooms in a large mixing bowl and gently toss with the $^1/_2$ cup of olive oil, the vinegar, and garlic; season to taste with salt and pepper. Take care the mushrooms don't break. Set aside to marinate for 20 to 30 minutes, tossing occasionally.
2. Prepare a charcoal or gas grill; the coals or heating elements should be medium hot. Lightly spray the grilling rack with vegetable oil spray to prevent sticking. Or, preheat the broiler or a stovetop grill.
3. Grill the mushrooms for 2 to 3 minutes on each side, or until cooked through. Let them rest for about 5 minutes before cutting each mushroom into 4 or 5 slices. Reserve the marinade to drizzle on the panini before grilling, if desired.
4. Using a pastry brush, lightly butter both sides of the bread. Set 4 slices aside.
5. Top each of the 4 slices with 2 tablespoons of Goat Cheese Spread and then with mushroom slices. Season to taste with salt and pepper. Drizzle with a little reserved marinade, if desired. Top with the remaining 4 slices of bread.

6. Heat a teaspoon or so of olive oil in a small skillet over medium-high heat or brush a panini press with olive oil and preheat to high. Grill each sandwich in the skillet for 2 to 3 minutes on each side, until the bread is golden brown and the cheese melts. Press the sandwich with a spatula when you turn it over. If you use a panini press, grill the sandwiches for about 8 minutes, or until the bread is golden brown and the cheese melts.

7. Cut each sandwich into rectangles and slice the rectangles into bricks, or bars, each about 1 inch long. Stack on plates and drizzle with a little truffle oil, if desired.

about the wine

This hearty sandwich is made rich by the almost meatlike portobellos and the creamy Goat Cheese Spread. Here, the grilled mushrooms can stand up to one of southern Italy's big guns: Aglianico. Grown mostly in Basilicata and Campania, the Aglianico grape is often compared to the Nebbiolo grape of Piedmont, because of their mutual ability to produce big, sophisticated reds with a notable capacity to age. We love the Aglianico del Vulture from Re Manfredi and Cantina del Notaio in Basilicata.

goat cheese spread | makes about 1 cup

1 cup softened goat cheese
1 tablespoon torn fresh basil
1 tablespoon chopped fresh flat-leaf parsley
1 tablespoon chopped fresh dill
1 tablespoon extra virgin olive oil
1 teaspoon honey
1 teaspoon crushed red pepper flakes
Kosher salt and cracked black pepper

1. In the bowl of an electric mixer fitted with the whip attachment, whip the goat cheese just until lightened. Add the basil, parsley, dill, olive oil, honey, and red pepper and whip until blended. Season to taste with salt and black pepper.

2. If not using immediately, transfer to a lidded container and refrigerate for up to 3 days. Let the spread come to room temperature before using.

Customers who have followed my career know that regardless of where I cook, they can count on finding three of my favorite indulgences on the menu: caviar, foie gras, and truffles. For this panini, I turn to truffles, the heady, earthy, and seductive tuber that is considered one of nature's finest treasures. There is no way around it: Truffles are costly, so I always suggest you use only as much as you can afford (without going overboard . . . although I find that hardly possible). I make a glorious egg and bacon panini with fresh or canned truffles and a few drops of intense white truffle oil. Both transform this very good yet ordinary breakfast sandwich into a panini fit for a king. Or, as I prefer, fit for my kids. Our time together is the morning, so we tend to eat big breakfasts as a family whenever we can. The boys love the scrambled eggs for this panini, and with the truffles I am introducing them to the finer things in life. It truly is a breakfast of champions!

truffled scrambled egg and bacon panini | *serves 4*

8 slices bacon
8 large eggs
$^1/4$ cup heavy cream
1 tablespoon chopped fresh or canned truffles (or as much as you can afford)
1 tablespoon chopped fresh chives
1 teaspoon white truffle oil
Kosher salt and cracked black pepper
1 tablespoon unsalted butter
4 tablespoons ($^1/2$ stick) salted butter, softened, for brushing
Eight $^1/2$-inch-thick slices ciabatta or Italian country-style bread
1 to 2 teaspoons olive oil
2 tablespoons freshly grated Parmigiano-Reggiano cheese

1. In a skillet set over medium heat, cook the bacon until crisp. Drain on paper towels and set aside.
2. In a large mixing bowl, whisk the eggs. Add the cream, truffles, chives, and $^1/2$ teaspoon of the truffle oil. Season with salt and pepper and whisk until frothy.
3. In a nonstick sauté pan set over medium heat, melt the tablespoon of unsalted butter with the remaining truffle oil. When the butter foams, pour in the egg mixture and cook, stirring constantly with a rubber spatula, until the eggs are soft but set. Do not overcook. *(continued)*

this varietal, often the least expensive and most simply bottled are the best for daily enjoyment. One of Chef Tramonto's favorites is the Dievole Pinocchio Nero d'Avola. It is a spicy, dark, fruited red with supple tannins, and it is just the thing for a panini that is, when all is said and done, a ham and cheese sandwich!

mustard mayonnaise | makes about $^2/_3$ cup

$^1/_2$ cup mayonnaise
2 tablespoons Dijon mustard
$1^1/_2$ teaspoons chopped fresh tarragon
1 teaspoon fresh lemon juice
Kosher salt and freshly ground black pepper

In a mixing bowl, whisk together the mayonnaise, mustard, tarragon, and lemon juice. Season to taste with salt and pepper. Use immediately or cover and refrigerate for up to 3 days.

CHAPTER 8

cicchetti

mini venetian-style
sandwiches

I

admire how Italians respect

sandwiches. Amble down any street in Italy and

your eye is drawn to small storefronts with great-looking

sandwiches displayed in glass cases, each one more appetizing than

the last: moist, fresh ham; juicy tomatoes; fried eggplant; and creamy,

farmstead cheese peeking out from between slices of crusty bakery bread or soft

rolls. Even if you've just polished off a plate of pasta, you flirt with the idea of

buying one of those gems! I know I do. This passion is seen throughout Europe, where

small, fastidiously composed sandwiches get the royal treatment. Americans know how to

make a good sandwich, too, as attested to by our renowned delis, but rarely do I see the small,

almost bite-sized sandwiches made with the gastronomic thoughtfulness of these little *cicchetti*.

For these eight sandwiches, I begin with one of two kinds of bread: soft torpedo rolls or crusty

Italian rolls. Torpedo rolls, as their name suggests, are elongated and so soft your teeth sink into them

effortlessly. There's no work; just the pleasure of your taste buds discovering fillings such as fatty,

rich foie gras; smoked salmon draped in lemony butter; and tender Gorgonzola dolce cheese mingling

with its best friend, a ripe pear. If you can't find good-quality torpedo rolls, use baguettes or brioche

rolls instead. The crusty Italian bread, which can be sourdough or not, is better suited to the brasher

fillings—the tuna conserva that, along with the tuna, serves up olives, capers, and cornichons.

ABOUT THE WINE

*Do as the Venetians do! Put your party in the mood, belly up to your bar, have a sandwich, and drink
the wines of the Veneto. With wine production centered in Verona, the Veneto is the third-largest
wine-producing region in Italy, and the largest in the north. Here you'll find elegant,
sophisticated, cool-climate viticulture; the refreshing sparkler, Prosecco; and a little
decadence as well with red wines such as Valpolicella and Amarone. We
particularly love the finesse of producers like Bele Casel, Nino Franco,
Vignalta, Puiatti, Cavalchina, and La Bionda. We enjoy the
blockbuster reds like Allegrini, Quintarelli, and
Dal Forno.*

For this gorgeous sandwich, find very high-quality smoked salmon (you don't want it too salty) and slice it just thin enough to drape over your hand without tearing. This is not quite paper-thin, which makes the salmon so fragile you have to wrestle with it, but skinny enough to be elegant and still have good flavor. Once you are satisfied with the salmon, slice the green tomatoes very thin. I am a fan of green tomatoes, but they have to be cut thin so they have a pickley flavor with just a little crunch and acidity. Think of them as playing the same role with the salmon as cornichons and cracked pepper. When you introduce these first-rate ingredients to the lemony butter and soft bread, you have a winner.

smoked salmon and green tomato with lemon butter cicchetti | *serves 4*

2 tablespoons unsalted butter, softened
$^1/2$ teaspoon fresh lemon juice
$^1/2$ teaspoon grated lemon zest
$^1/2$ teaspoon chopped fresh chives
$^1/2$ teaspoon chopped fresh tarragon
Kosher salt and cracked black pepper
Four 3- to 4-inch-long soft-crusted torpedo rolls
4 ounces smoked salmon, thinly sliced
4 thin slices green tomato (1 small tomato)

1. In a mixing bowl, mash together the butter, lemon juice and zest, chives, and tarragon. Season to taste with salt and pepper. Mix until the butter is smooth and creamy.
2. Split the torpedo rolls horizontally. Spread about $1^1/2$ teaspoons of the butter on both halves. Top each with salmon and a tomato slice. Sandwich with the top half, close the rolls gently, and serve at room temperature.

about the wine

A simple, minimally- or unoaked Chardonnay from the Veneto is the best bet here. The zippy green tomatoes, salmon, and lemon butter benefit from an equivalent level of acidity in the wine, and from the echo of the citrus in the cool-climate Chardonnay. Dal Bello is one of the Chardonnays that we pour in our restaurants, and there are others in this same style.

The food press has written about my commitment to foie gras, which has been on my menu for more than ten years and become one of my signatures. Unfortunately, there has been a lot of controversy about foie gras in recent years—and even bans on serving it—which I believe is a shame. I wouldn't dream of letting a piece of foie gras go to waste and sometimes make a paste from the scraps to snack on at work. For this *cicchetti*, I use prepared foie gras or foie gras pâté or mousse, which is sold in gourmet stores. I whip it into a paste to make a sandwich that is pure indulgence and a great little bite when you're waiting for the pasta water to boil. Go for it!

creamy foie gras cicchetti | *serves 4*

^{1}/2 cup prepared foie gras, preferably a smooth pâté or mousse
8 tablespoons (1 stick) unsalted butter, softened
1^1/2 teaspoons fresh orange juice
1 teaspoon port wine
1 tablespoon chopped fresh flat-leaf parsley
1 teaspoon grated orange zest
Kosher salt
Cracked pink or black peppercorns
Four 3- to 4-inch-long soft-crusted torpedo rolls or length of baguette

1. In the bowl of an electric mixer fitted with the paddle attachment and set on medium speed, mix the foie gras and butter until smooth.
2. Add the orange juice, wine, parsley, and orange zest and mix until well blended. Season to taste with salt and pepper.
3. Split the torpedo rolls horizontally but do not cut all the way through. Spread approximately 2 tablespoons of the foie gras in each roll. Close the rolls gently and serve at room temperature.

about the wine

Sweet wine and foie gras are a classic pairing. A fun way to respect this tradition is to pair this *cicchetti* with a sweet Garganega from the Veneto. Soave producer Ca'Rugate bottles the gently sweet "Bucciato da Uve Garganega," and it knocks our socks off! Floral, honeyed, and succulent, this wine might make you forget about the bottle of Sauternes that you typically set aside for foie gras.

Seafood salad is my favorite snack food or light meal. I love it made with shrimp, but won't turn down a salad made with crabmeat or even salmon. Seafood must be pristinely fresh. Buy the best shrimp you can find and if you can't find any of high quality or you prefer, substitute lobster or crab. Like the other recipes in the book, this one is all about the ingredients, so splurge a little and get the very finest.

shrimp salad cicchetti | *serves 4*

$1/2$ pound peeled, cooked shrimp, diced (about 2 cups)
$1/2$ cup homemade or store-bought mayonnaise
$1/4$ cup finely diced celery
2 tablespoons finely diced red onion
2 tablespoons fresh lemon juice
1 tablespoon Dijon mustard
1 tablespoon finely chopped fresh flat-leaf parsley
1 tablespoon finely chopped fresh tarragon
1 teaspoon grated lemon zest
$1/2$ teaspoon cayenne
Kosher salt and cracked black pepper
Four 3- to 4-inch-long crusty Italian rolls or length of baguette
$1/4$ cup chiffonade (finely shredded) romaine lettuce

1. In a bowl, mix the shrimp, mayonnaise, celery, onion, lemon juice, mustard, parsley, tarragon, lemon zest, and cayenne. Season to taste with salt and black pepper.
2. Split the rolls horizontally. Mound 2 to 3 tablespoons of the shrimp mixture on the bottom half of each roll. Top with romaine and the other half of each roll. Cut the sandwiches in half.
3. Wrap each sandwich tightly in wax paper. They are messy and the wax paper will make them easier to serve and to eat. Serve at room temperature.

about the wine

A white with attitude like Lugana (an appellation that straddles both the Veneto and Lombardy) is the right wine to pour with this elegant shrimp salad *cicchetti*. When it comes to this style of wine, the star of the Veneto is Zenato, and their Trebbiano-based Lugana wines, made from vineyards overlooking Lake Garda, will not disappoint.

I took a classic cheese course and turned it into a sandwich, with just a drizzle of honey to gently wake up the flavors. I love Gorgonzola dolce with this, but if you have another high-quality Gorgonzola in mind, go for it. The other crucial ingredient is the pear, which should be perfectly ripe. Make sure they give when pressed and are sweetly fragrant.

gorgonzola with pear cicchetti | *serves 4*

$3/4$ cup Gorgonzola dolce, softened (see Note, page 36)
2 tablespoons heavy cream
$1^1/2$ teaspoons extra virgin olive oil
1 tablespoon chopped fresh chives
Cracked black pepper
Four 3- to 4-inch-long soft-crusted torpedo rolls
1 ripe pear, such as Bosc or Anjou, peeled, cored, and thinly sliced
$1/2$ cup roasted walnuts, finely chopped (see Note)
1 tablespoon chestnut or other mild honey

1. In the bowl of an electric mixer fitted with the paddle attachment and set on medium speed, mix the Gorgonzola, cream, olive oil, and chives until smooth and creamy. Season to taste with pepper and mix again.
2. Split the torpedo rolls horizontally but do not cut all the way through. Spread approximately 3 tablespoons of the Gorgonzola on each roll.
3. Top each roll with a few pear slices and chopped walnuts. Drizzle with honey, close the rolls gently, and serve at room temperature.

NOTE To roast walnuts, spread them in a dry skillet and toast over medium-high heat, shaking the pan gently, for 5 to 10 minutes, until they are fragrant and darken a shade. Or, place them on a baking sheet and roast in a 375°F oven for 10 to 12 minutes, stirring occasionally, until fragrant and slightly darkened. Let the nuts cool before chopping.

about the wine

We have used every excuse in the book to open a bottle of one of Quintarelli's wines, and we are giving you one, too. You need a fruit bomb to bring together this blue cheese sandwich with fruit and nuts, and Quintarelli's uber-decadent, almost Amarone, Valpolicella is it. This Valpolicella has a luxurious, plush texture and gobs of ripe, candied, stewed fruit character.

There are little sandwich shops all over Italy, as well as New York and Las Vegas, and one memorable place in the Venetian Hotel in Las Vegas makes very cool little sandwiches. Many of them are wrapped in tissue paper, befitting the little culinary gems that they are. I grabbed one when staying there, and was "grabbed" by the farmstead ricotta cheese. Fresh Italian ricotta is amazing, but it is not always available. Luckily, more and more American cheese producers are turning out artisanal ricotta that rivals the best from Italy. Farmstead ricotta is mildly sweet with nutty overtones and a pleasing texture—not bland, but full flavored.

fresh ricotta and sun-dried
tomato cicchetti | *serves 4*

12 or 13 ounces fresh ricotta

^{1}/4 cup drained, julienned oil-packed sun-dried tomatoes

2 tablespoons freshly grated Parmigiano-Reggiano cheese

1 tablespoon extra virgin olive oil

1 tablespoon torn fresh basil

1 tablespoon minced fresh chives

1 teaspoon fresh lemon juice

Kosher salt and cracked black pepper

Four 3- to 4-inch-long soft-crusted torpedo rolls

1. Line a sieve with cheesecloth and set it over a bowl. Put the ricotta in the sieve, refrigerate, and let drain for about 1 hour or until relatively dry. You should have about 1 cup of drained ricotta.
2. Transfer the cheese to a mixing bowl and add the tomatoes, cheese, olive oil, basil, chives, and lemon juice. Whisk until well mixed. Season to taste with salt and pepper.
3. Split the torpedo rolls horizontally but do not cut all the way through. Spread approximately 2 to 3 tablespoons of the ricotta mixture into each roll. Close the rolls gently and serve at room temperature.

about the wine

The ultrafresh and clean flavor from the ricotta dictates that the accompanying wine be a clean style as well. Crisp, racy Prosecco is the right choice for this *cicchetti*. Many wine bars in the Veneto subtly (or not so subtly) nudge almost every guest in the direction of Prosecco.

My mother's father, Vincenzo Gentile, was one of the few people who called me Ricky. He was a barber who emigrated from Abruzzi to Rochester, New York, and brought with him many of the customs of his homeland. One was to eat spicy coppa salumi with just about everything! Vincenzo hacked off pieces of coppa and pecorino cheese and wrapped them in thin slices of bread. He ate these mini sandwiches morning, afternoon, or evening—he even dunked them in his coffee! And so, in honor of my grandfather, I developed this little sandwich. Very few ingredients, but if you buy freshly baked bread, good, firm coppa, and great cheese, you can't go wrong. You have Vincenzo's word! "*Buono,* Ricky!"

coppa and pecorino toscano cicchetti | *serves 4*

Four 3- to 4-inch-long crusty Italian rolls or baguette
12 thin slices coppa (see Note)
4 thin slices pecorino Toscano cheese
8 fresh basil leaves
2 tablespoons extra virgin olive oil
Cracked black pepper

1. Split the rolls horizontally but do not cut all the way through.
2. Put 3 slices of coppa on each sandwich and top with a slice of cheese and 2 basil leaves.
3. Drizzle each sandwich with olive oil and season to taste with pepper. Close the rolls gently and serve at room temperature.

NOTE Sienna is best known for coppa, which is cut from the pork shoulder, salted, flavored, and then dry-cured for at least six months. The result is a tender, wonderfully flavorful meat.

about the wine

Coffee works here, but we like this *cicchetti* even better with Valpolicella. Generations of savvy winemakers have combined the Corvina, Rondinella, and Molinara grapes to create this wine known as "baby Amarone." A cleaner style from a classic producer like La Bionda will reward you with pristine fruit in a wine that is aromatic and intense.

CHAPTER 9

antipasti

little plates
before the pasta

I
love antipasti and my family was
great at making them. If I wanted to be literal, I
would tell you to serve any one of the following twenty-one
dishes before you serve pasta. But that doesn't interest me. Yes, any
would be great before a pasta course, but each stands on its own as a small
plate that has been inspired by my Italian heritage. These are not necessarily
Italian, although the Tuscan Panzanella and Pappa Pomodoro are about as authentic as
you can get. But how about the garlicky lobster, glazed carrots, or parsnips with
cranberries? These recipes are among my favorites and some were slotted in this chapter
because, frankly, they didn't quite fit anywhere else—but they had to be in the book.
I view this chapter as running the gamut from simple to sophisticated, light to more substantial,
traditional to innovative. I have even included a soup, the only one in the book. Many of these
recipes could be enlarged to become a meal (think of the steamed mussels, frittata with prosciutto, and
polenta with meat ragu) while others could be shrunk to become a passed hors d'oeuvre (try the
swordfish roll-ups, crusted calamari, or rice balls). And still others would make lovely side dishes and
salads, such as the white beans with tomatoes, cauliflower with raisins, and cucumber salad. But
whether you serve them as originally intended, as a small plate with a glass of great wine, or some
other way, they are unbeatable! Just a reminder: As I explained in Chapter 1, I have not included
individual wine notes with these recipes and those in Chapter 10, "Cheese." Instead, the umbrella
note at the beginning of the chapter will guide you.

ABOUT THE WINE

In restaurants, those little plates can cause your sommelier or wine steward sleepless nights and
endless consternation. What to pour when every flavor, spice, vegetable, fish, and meat under
the sun can be crafted and served as antipasti? We have found that the "Terminator"
wine of the antipasti dilemma is the pink stuff! Bardolino Chiaretto, Aglianico
Rosato, Rosato of Negroamaro—north, south, east, west, you will find
the dry Italian rosé that you love best! Pour them with all
of these and you can't go wrong.

My son Gio cooks with me all the time. He was asked to make a frittata on a kids' Webcast called Spatulatta.com, so he and I worked together to hone his skill and come up with a recipe that was fun and a little challenging. Gio shares my love for artichokes, and the angel hair pasta not only makes this "Italian" by replacing the potatoes in traditional Spanish frittatas, but stabilizes the dish so it's easy to work with. There's nothing kidlike about the flavors rich with Parmigiano-Reggiano cheese, cream, and fresh herbs; everyone will love this! And, if I do say so, Gio was a natural in front of the camera. Made me proud!

angel hair frittata with artichokes and black pepper pecorino | *serves 4*

$^1/2$ pound angel hair pasta

12 large eggs

$^1/4$ cup freshly grated Parmigiano-Reggiano cheese

2 tablespoons heavy cream

$1^1/2$ teaspoons chopped fresh flat-leaf parsley

$1^1/2$ teaspoons chopped fresh basil

$1^1/2$ teaspoons chopped fresh tarragon

Kosher salt and cracked black pepper

2 tablespoons olive oil

1 cup thinly sliced yellow onions

1 teaspoon minced garlic

1 cup quartered artichokes, either fresh cooked; canned in brine, drained; or thawed frozen

2 tablespoons unsalted butter

$^1/4$ cup sour cream or crème frâiche

$^1/3$ cup shaved black pepper pecorino cheese

1. Preheat the oven to 350°F.
2. Bring a large saucepan of lightly salted water to a boil and cook the pasta according to package directions until al dente. Drain.
3. In a mixing bowl, whisk together the eggs, Parmigiano-Reggiano, cream, parsley, basil, and tarragon, and season to taste with salt and pepper. Add the pasta, toss to mix, and set aside for about 3 minutes to give the pasta time to absorb as much of the egg mixture as possible.

4. Heat a large ovenproof nonstick skillet over medium-high heat and when hot, pour in the oil. Add the onions and cook for about 3 minutes, just until wilted. Add the garlic and artichokes and cook for about 2 minutes, stirring, until well mixed.

5. Add the butter to the pan and when it melts, lift the pasta from the bowl and pile it in the skillet. Spoon enough of the remaining egg mixture over the top to cover the pasta.

6. Cook over medium heat, occasionally stirring gently, until the egg starts to firm up. Transfer to the oven and cook for 5 to 7 minutes, or until the bottom of the frittata is golden brown when gently lifted.

7. Slide the frittata from the pan onto a cutting board and let it rest for 3 to 5 minutes.

8. Cut into 4 wedges and put each one on a small plate. Top each with 1 tablespoon of sour cream, or spoon it next to the frittata. Garnish with pecorino.

A grain-based antipasto makes all kinds of sense to me, and a little plate is a great way to introduce people to farro, which might be unfamiliar. The grain absorbs the stock much like rice does in risotto, and becomes nice and creamy—the ideal foundation for the sautéed vegetables. I love to make this with summer vegetables, but you could use other veggies, depending on the season.

farro with vegetables | *serves 4*

FARRO

2 tablespoons unsalted butter

$^3/_4$ cup finely diced onions

1 cup uncooked whole-grain farro (see Note)

2 quarts chicken or vegetable stock

Kosher salt and freshly ground black pepper

VEGETABLES

$^1/_4$ cup olive oil

1 tablespoon slivered garlic

12 pearl onions, blanched

$^1/_2$ cup diced fennel

$^1/_2$ cup sliced slender green beans (also called French beans)

$^1/_3$ cup diced zucchini

$^1/_3$ cup diced yellow squash

$^3/_4$ cup corn kernels (about 1 ear)

16 red and yellow cherry tomatoes, halved

$^1/_2$ cup Kalamata olives, pitted and quartered

$^1/_4$ cup julienned fresh basil

Kosher salt and freshly ground black pepper

$^1/_2$ cup freshly grated Parmigiano-Reggiano cheese

3 tablespoons unsalted butter

1 tablespoon sherry vinegar

$^1/_2$ cup extra virgin olive oil

1 tablespoon chopped fresh flat-leaf parsley

$^1/_2$ cup shaved Parmigiano-Reggiano cheese

browned. Remove the octopus from the grill and cut into $^1/_2$-inch-long pieces. Leave the tentacles whole and set aside for garnish. Transfer the octopus to a mixing bowl.

5. Cut the potatoes into $^1/_4$-inch slices and add to the bowl with the octopus. Add the bell peppers, the vinaigrette, vinegar, 4 tablespoons of the parsley, the garlic, oregano, and red pepper. Toss and season to taste with salt and black pepper.

6. Set aside to marinate at room temperature for at least 30 minutes but no longer than 1 hour.

7. Divide the octopus salad among 4 plates. Drizzle with olive oil, check the seasonings, and garnish with the remaining parsley and the tentacles.

baby octopus | makes 2 to 2$^1/_2$ pounds

1 cup white wine vinegar
2 yellow onions, cut into large dice
2 carrots, cut into large dice
4 garlic cloves, crushed
2 sprigs fresh flat-leaf parsley
2 sprigs fresh thyme
1$^1/_2$ teaspoons crushed red pepper flakes
1 bay leaf
$^1/_3$ cup kosher salt
1$^1/_2$ teaspoons black peppercorns
2 to 2$^1/_2$ pounds baby octopus, heads and beaks removed
$^1/_2$ cup extra virgin olive oil

1. Fill a large stockpot with 4 quarts (1 gallon) of water. Add the vinegar, onions, carrots, garlic, parsley, thyme, red pepper, bay leaf, and salt. Bring to a boil over medium-high heat and boil for 45 minutes.

2. Add the peppercorns and boil for 15 minutes longer. Drain, reserving the court bouillon (liquid) and discarding the vegetables.

3. Return the court bouillon to the pot and bring to a boil over medium-high heat. Add the octopus, reduce to a brisk simmer, and cook for 30 minutes. Remove from the heat and let the octopus cool in the liquid for 1 hour.

4. Drain the octopus, discarding the liquid. Transfer the octopus to a dish and coat with the olive oil. If not using right away, cover and refrigerate for up to 24 hours. (continued)

herb oil | makes about 2^1/2 cups

1 bunch fresh flat-leaf parsley
2^1/2 cups grapeseed oil
4 ounces fresh chives
4 ounces fresh tarragon
4 ounces fresh chervil
2 tablespoons kosher salt

1. Remove the parsley leaves from the stems. Discard the stems.
2. In a large sauté pan, heat ^{1}/4 cup of the grapeseed oil over high heat. When hot, add the parsley, chives, tarragon, and chervil. Sauté for about 2 minutes, or until the herbs are wilted. Season with the salt. Transfer to a plate and let cool.
3. When cool, transfer the herbs to a blender. With the motor running, slowly add the remaining oil and blend for 2 to 3 minutes.
4. Transfer to a glass container and cover. Let the herbs steep in the refrigerator overnight or up to 24 hours.
5. Strain the oil through a chinois or fine-mesh sieve into a small bowl or glass container. Cover and refrigerate for up to 2 days.

lemon vinaigrette | makes about 2 cups

1 cup extra virgin olive oil
^{2}/3 cup fresh lemon juice
^{1}/2 cup white wine vinegar
4 teaspoons Dijon mustard
1 shallot, minced
Kosher salt and freshly ground white pepper

1. In a blender, combine the olive oil, lemon juice, vinegar, mustard, and shallot. Blend until thoroughly emulsified. Season to taste with salt and pepper.
2. Use immediately or cover and refrigerate for up to 1 week. Let come to room temperature and whisk well before using.

When I visited land-locked Umbria, the region just southeast of Tuscany, I gazed upward and understood Michelangelo's inspiration for the heavenly skies that graced his art. Not quite as stirring, perhaps, but nevertheless memorable, was a potato and spinach frittata I shared with a local family after church one Sunday. I think it's the recollection of the day, the sky, and the warm hospitality of my Umbrian friends that encouraged me to make a similar frittata. Whatever the reason, I am glad I did. I think you will be, too. Serve this warm or at room temperature; the latter may be easier for an antipasto.

frittata with prosciutto, potato, and spinach | *serves 4*

One large russet potato (about 7 ounces)
1 cup packed stemmed fresh spinach
$^1/_4$ cup olive oil
$^1/_2$ yellow onion, diced
2 garlic cloves, minced
Kosher salt and freshly ground black pepper
6 large eggs
$^1/_4$ cup heavy cream
$^1/_4$ cup freshly grated Parmigiano-Reggiano cheese
$^1/_4$ cup freshly grated Gruyère or provolone cheese
2 ounces prosciutto, sliced and coarsely chopped
2 tablespoons chopped fresh basil
4 teaspoons sour cream
2 tablespoons chopped fresh flat-leaf parsley
Extra virgin olive oil

1. Bring a saucepan of lightly salted water to a boil over medium-high heat. Peel the potato and cut into $^1/_4$-inch cubes. Add the potatoes and cook for about 15 minutes, or until al dente. Drain.

2. Fill a skillet with water to a depth of $^1/_2$ inch. Rinse the spinach well and transfer to the skillet. Bring to a boil over medium-high heat and cook just until the spinach begins to wilt. Do not cook until completely wilted. Lift the spinach from the pan, squeeze out excess moisture, and chop.

(continued)

3. In a heavy, ovenproof skillet, heat the olive oil over medium heat. Add the potato, onion, and garlic. Season with salt and pepper and sauté for 3 to 4 minutes, or until the potatoes are golden and crisp on the outside and tender on the inside. Add the spinach and sauté for 1 to 2 minutes, or until the potatoes and spinach are well mixed and the spinach wilts a little more. Remove from the heat.

4. Preheat the broiler.

5. In a nonreactive bowl, whisk together the eggs, cream, Parmesan and Gruyère, prosciutto, and basil. Pour into the potato-spinach mixture and cook over medium-low heat for about 3 minutes, until the eggs are nearly set but the top is still liquid and loose. Put the skillet under the broiler and cook for about 4 minutes, until the top is set and golden brown.

6. Using a rubber spatula, loosen the frittata from the skillet and slide it onto a cutting board. Cut into 8 wedges.

7. Put 2 wedges on each of 4 plates. Garnish each wedge with sour cream and parsley and a drizzle of olive oil.

Small and silvery, smelts can be cooked and eaten whole, and as delicious as they are simply pan-seared, when you deep-fry and serve them with a garlicky, caper-studded aioli, they are beyond fantastic! You can cook smelts with the heads on or not, but regardless, they are only about six inches long. Although native to the North Atlantic, they were introduced to the Great Lakes early in the last century and have thrived ever since. From Maine to Illinois, when smelts leave the protection of a cold, deep ocean or lake to spawn in small streams and tributaries, they signal springtime. Schools of smelts swim along the coastlines on their way to their spawning grounds, and sport fishermen are permitted to toss nets in the water to haul them out by the thousands. If you can't find smelts for this recipe, use herring instead.

fried smelts with caper aioli | *serves 4*

AIOLI

3 cups homemade or high-quality store-bought mayonnaise

4 garlic cloves, coarsely chopped

Juice of 2 lemons

3 tablespoons drained, coarsely chopped capers

$^{1}/_{4}$ cup chopped fresh flat-leaf parsley

1 teaspoon cayenne

Sea salt and freshly ground black pepper

SMELTS

1 pound fresh cleaned smelts or herring

1 cup all-purpose flour

1 tablespoon garlic powder

1 tablespoon paprika

$1^{1}/_{2}$ teaspoons cayenne

$1^{1}/_{2}$ teaspoons onion powder

$1^{1}/_{2}$ teaspoons dried oregano

1 teaspoon kosher salt, plus more for seasoning

1 teaspoon cracked black pepper, plus more for seasoning

About $^{1}/_{2}$ gallon canola oil

1 lemon, quartered

2 tablespoons chopped fresh flat-leaf parsley

1. *To prepare the aioli:* In a mixing bowl, stir together the mayonnaise, garlic, lemon juice, capers, parsley, and cayenne. Set aside for at least 10 minutes and up to 30 minutes to give the flavors time to blend. (If not using right away, cover and refrigerate.) Taste and season with salt and black pepper.

2. *To prepare the smelts:* Rinse in cold water and wipe completely dry. (If not using right away, wrap in plastic and refrigerate until needed.)

3. In a shallow dish, mix the flour, garlic powder, paprika, cayenne, onion powder, oregano, salt, and black pepper.

4. Pour oil into a deep, heavy pot or Dutch oven to a depth of 6 inches. Using a deep-frying thermometer to determine temperature, heat the oil to 350°F over high heat. Moderate the heat to maintain the temperature.

5. Meanwhile, dredge the fish in the flour mixture, coating completely on both sides.

6. Gently lower a few fish into the oil until fully submerged. Deep-fry for about 4 minutes, or until cooked through. Turn with tongs to ensure even browning. Lift from the oil, set aside to drain on paper towels, and season with salt and black pepper. Repeat with the remaining smelts. Do not crowd the pan, and let the oil regain its heat between batches.

7. Put the smelts on a serving platter. Garnish the platter with lemon wedges and parsley. Serve the aioli in a separate bowl for dipping.

My mom made green bean salads all summer as long as the beans were in season, and I have always loved them. I sampled a yellow and green bean salad at a huge food and wine market in Milan called Peck, a large, three-story establishment that includes a restaurant and a casual Italian bar that's open from early morning through early evening. The salad was made with olives, so it reminded me of my mother's green bean salad taken to the next level. My version relies on a sherry vinaigrette that, if I do say so myself, makes this little plate *fantastico!*

green and yellow beans with
sherry vinaigrette | *serves 4*

$^1/4$ cup extra virgin olive oil

2 tablespoons sherry vinegar

1 tablespoon minced shallot

1 tablespoon torn fresh basil leaves

$1^1/2$ teaspoons honey

Kosher salt and cracked black pepper

2 tablespoons pitted and slivered black Cerignola olives

2 tablespoons pitted and slivered green Cerignola olives

$^3/4$ pound green beans, trimmed and left whole

$^3/4$ pound yellow wax beans, trimmed and left whole

2 tablespoons shaved Parmigiano-Reggiano cheese

1. In a large bowl, whisk together the oil, vinegar, shallot, basil, and honey; season to taste with salt and pepper. Stir in the olives.
2. Bring a saucepan of lightly salted water to a boil and blanch the green and yellow beans for about 3 minutes, or until crisp-tender. Drain and then plunge into a large bowl of ice water to stop the cooking. Drain again.
3. Add the beans to the bowl with the vinaigrette and toss. Season to taste with salt and pepper. Divide among 4 plates and garnish with the cheese.

A good bread salad soaks up the juices from the tomatoes, olive oil, vinegar, and all the other seductive flavors that go into a really top-flight panzanella, and I love it! The tomatoes should be at their juicy, high-summer peak and the bread bakery-fresh, with a pleasingly soft crumb and chewy crust. My recipe not only calls for the best tomatoes and bread, but also relies on green, fruity, extra virgin olive oil, zesty red wine vinegar, salty capers, and freshly grated lemon zest. (I use a microplane when I zest citrus fruit and I highly recommend you do the same.) I also add other vegetables such as red onion, bell peppers, and fennel, garden-fresh basil, and some inky black olives for a salad bursting with summer.

tuscan panzanella | *serves 4*

4 cups torn pieces of sourdough or rustic peasant bread,
    1 to 1^1/2 inches wide
3 tablespoons olive oil
Kosher salt and cracked black pepper
^{1}/4 cup red wine vinegar
1 tablespoon drained capers
2 teaspoons grated lemon zest
1 garlic clove, minced
^{1}/2 cup extra virgin olive oil
1 cup thinly sliced red onion
5 assorted ripe heirloom tomatoes, halved or quartered,
    depending on size and shape
1 red bell pepper, julienned
1 yellow bell pepper, julienned
1 cucumber, peeled, seeded, and chopped
1 fennel bulb, trimmed and thinly sliced, fronds reserved
^{1}/2 cup pitted and halved Niçoise olives
^{1}/4 cup chopped fresh basil leaves
^{1}/4 cup shaved Parmigiano-Reggiano cheese

1. Preheat the oven to 300°F.
2. In a bowl, toss the bread with the olive oil and salt and pepper to taste. Spread the bread on a baking sheet and bake for 7 to 10 minutes, until slightly crisp. (The pieces should not be as

crispy as croutons.) Alternatively, spread the bread cubes on a baking sheet and let them dry, uncovered, for about 24 hours.

3. In a large bowl, whisk together the vinegar, capers, zest, and garlic. Season to taste with salt and pepper. Whisking constantly, add the extra virgin olive oil in a stream until well incorporated.

4. Add the onion, tomatoes, bell peppers, cucumber, fennel, and olives and toss with the vinaigrette. Adjust the salt and pepper.

5. Tear the fennel fronds and add them to the bowl along with the basil and bread. Toss to coat. Set aside for 20 minutes.

6. Divide the salad among 4 plates. Garnish each plate with shaved cheese and serve. If you prefer a moister salad, drizzle with a little more extra virgin olive oil.

If you have never cooked a spaghetti squash, don't wait another minute. The flesh of the mild squash magically turns into strands when it's cooked, hence its name. On the other hand, if you prefer, make this wonderful little antipasto with any winter squash, such as butternut or acorn. The flavors of the orange, cinnamon, and butter come together in a tantalizing aromatic symphony, and you, as the cook, will get a standing ovation! Serve it as an antipasto or a side dish. Either way, it's a masterpiece.

roasted spaghetti squash with vanilla and marcona almonds | *serves 4*

1 orange
$^1/_2$ pound (2 sticks) high-quality unsalted butter, softened (see Note, page 135)
2 teaspoons freshly grated nutmeg
Kosher salt and freshly ground black pepper
1 vanilla bean, split
1 spaghetti squash (2 to 3 pounds)
$^1/_3$ cup olive oil
2 tablespoons light or dark brown sugar
1 tablespoon chopped fresh thyme
2 cinnamon sticks
$^2/_3$ cup whole Marcona almonds

1. Preheat the oven to 375°F.
2. Working over a mixing bowl, use a microplane or box grater to grate the zest of 1 orange. Add the butter and mash to mix. Stir in the nutmeg and lightly season to taste with salt and pepper. Scrape half of the vanilla bean seeds into the butter. Reserve the bean and the remaining seeds.
3. Split the squash in half lengthwise and scrape out all the seeds. Rub the exposed flesh with olive oil and season to taste with salt and pepper.
4. Put the squash cut side down in a roasting pan and bake for about 1 hour. Turn over and put $^1/_4$ cup of the orange-vanilla butter and the juice of half an orange in each side of the squash. Divide the brown sugar, thyme, cinnamon sticks, and reserved vanilla bean halves between the squash halves. *(continued)*

1. *To make the sauce:* Put the lemon juice in a small nonreactive bowl. Add the olive oil in a slow, steady stream, whisking until emulsified. Stir in the parsley, basil, capers, and rosemary and season to taste with salt and pepper. Set aside until ready to use. Whisk before using.

2. *To make the fish:* Lay the swordfish between 2 sheets of plastic wrap. Using a meat mallet or the bottom of a small, heavy skillet, lightly pound the fish until it is about $^1/_4$ inch thick. Transfer the fish to a plate, season with salt and black pepper.

3. Preheat the oven to 400°F.

4. In a sauté pan, heat 2 tablespoons of the olive oil over medium-high heat. Sauté the onion and garlic for 2 to 3 minutes, or until the onion is translucent. Add the bread crumbs and cook, stirring, for 2 to 3 minutes, or until golden brown. Remove pan from the heat and stir in the parsley, thyme, capers, and red pepper. Season with salt and black pepper and set aside.

5. Sprinkle the bread crumb mixture over the fish. Cover with the provolone and roll each piece of fish into a roll. Hold the rolls closed with toothpicks.

6. In an ovenproof sauté pan, heat 1 tablespoon of olive oil over medium heat and sauté the swordfish rolls until golden brown on all sides. Turn them carefully with tongs or a wooden spoon. Transfer the pan to the oven and bake for 4 to 6 minutes, just until they are still moist in the center. Do not overcook.

7. Put each swordfish roll on a plate. Whisk the vinaigrette and spoon a little over each roll. Garnish with any remaining bread crumbs.

If we take the time to listen to our grandparents' and great-grandparents' stories of survival during hard times, we can understand the genesis of many of the dishes we now consider traditional. Pappa pomodoro is a case in point. There are hundreds of ways to make this soup, whose primary ingredients are tomatoes and stale bread cooked until paplike (hence the word *pappa*). I raise the level of this so-called peasant food with careful seasoning and by finishing it with green, fruity olive oil and rich, salty cheese.

pappa pomodoro | *serves 4*

3 tablespoons olive oil

1 yellow onion, diced

1 garlic clove, minced

1 bay leaf

1 tablespoon crushed red pepper flakes

2 pounds tomatoes, peeled, cored, seeded, and roughly chopped, or two
    14-ounce cans diced tomatoes or one 28-ounce can crushed tomatoes

$3/4$ pound day-old (slightly stale) Italian bread, torn into 1-inch pieces

2 cups chicken stock, vegetable stock, or water

1 cup loosely packed, chopped fresh basil

$1/4$ cup extra virgin olive oil

Kosher salt and freshly ground black pepper

2 tablespoons unsalted butter

$1/4$ cup freshly grated Parmigiano-Reggiano cheese

1. In a large sauté pan, heat the olive oil over medium-high heat until hot but not smoking.
2. Add the onion, garlic, bay leaf, and red pepper and sauté for 2 to 3 minutes, or until softened.
3. Add the tomatoes and their juices and bring to a boil. Reduce the heat and simmer for about 5 minutes, until the tomatoes begin to soften and break down.
4. Put the bread slices in a bowl and cover with the stock. The bread will absorb much of the liquid right away. Transfer the bread and any liquid in the bowl to the sauté pan. Return to a simmer and cook for 8 to 10 minutes or until the bread has absorbed as much liquid as possible and is the consistency of soft baby food.
5. Stir in the basil, 3 tablespoons of the extra virgin olive oil, and salt and black pepper to taste. Cook the soup at a simmer for about 10 minutes to develop the flavors.
6. Stir the butter into the hot soup; when it's incorporated, ladle the soup into 4 shallow soup bowls. Garnish each serving with cheese and a drizzle of the remaining olive oil.

Sausage, roasted peppers, and onions are about as homestyle Italian as you can get. When I was growing up in Rochester, New York, my mother, grandmothers, and aunts carried big platters of these to the table as antipasti and I very happily dug in! Now that I live in Chicago, I buy tremendous sausage in the city's Italian neighborhoods, every bit as good as I remember from the old days. This dish is also traditional in Italy, particularly in the southern regions where the peppers and onions are so full-flavored and moist. A little farther north in the Chiana Valley, the pork is great; I tasted amazing pork sausage there. Buy the best Italian sausage you can possibly find and make sure everything else is at the peak of perfection. This dish is testimony to the reason for a lot of traditions: The food just tastes so good!

italian sausage with roasted peppers
and onions | *serves 4*

1/4 cup olive oil, plus more for oiling the pan
1 pound hot or sweet Italian sausage links
1 green bell pepper
1 red bell pepper
1 yellow bell pepper
1 large yellow onion, sliced
3 garlic cloves, chopped
1 teaspoon crushed red pepper flakes
3/4 cup chicken stock
1 tablespoon unsalted butter
2 tablespoons chopped fresh basil
Kosher salt and cracked black pepper
2 tablespoons freshly grated Parmigiano-Reggiano cheese

1. Preheat the oven to 400°F.
2. Lightly oil a shallow baking pan and roast the sausage for 10 to 15 minutes, until about three-quarters cooked. Turn occasionally during roasting to ensure even cooking. Remove the sausage from the oven but do not turn off the oven.
3. Meanwhile, slice the peppers into strips about 2 inches long and 1 inch wide. In a heavy,

ovenproof sauté pan, heat the olive oil over medium-high heat. When hot, sauté the onion, bell peppers, garlic, and red pepper for 4 to 6 minutes, or until the bell peppers begin to wilt.

4. Cut the sausage links into $1^1/2$- to 2-inch pieces. Add the sausages to the peppers and onion and stir to mix.

5. Pour the chicken stock into the sauté pan and put in the oven. Cook for 5 to 7 minutes or until the sausage is cooked through. Remove from the oven and swirl in the butter until incorporated. Stir in the basil and season to taste with salt and black pepper.

6. Divide among 4 plates and garnish with cheese.

I had never thought of combining steamed mussels with pepperoni until I was served this dish at a waterfront restaurant during a trip to Naples, Italy. It was a perfect sunny day and the perfectly cooked, fresh-from-the-sea mussels hit the spot. My interpretation makes a magnificent antipasti, whether served in shallow bowls or family style, on a platter. A real palate opener, which is what antipasti are all about!

steamed black mussels with garlic and spicy pepperoni | *serves 4*

^{1}/2 cup extra virgin olive oil
1 cup diced yellow onions
3 tablespoons chopped garlic
2 pounds black mussels, rinsed and scrubbed
^{1}/2 cup white wine
1 pound tomatoes, peeled, cored, seeded, and chopped
2 cups diced spicy pepperoni
3 tablespoons chopped fresh flat-leaf parsley
^{1}/4 cup anisette or ouzo
Kosher salt and cracked black pepper
2 tablespoons unsalted butter

1. In a large saucepan, heat the oil over medium-high heat. Add the onions and sauté for about 2 minutes, until tender but not colored. Add the garlic and sauté for 1 or 2 minutes longer, taking care the garlic does not burn.
2. Add the mussels, wine, tomatoes, pepperoni, and parsley. Stir well, bring to a boil, and cook for about 5 minutes, or until the mussels open. Discard any that do not open. With a large spoon, stir the contents of the pan.
3. Add the anisette or ouzo and season to taste with salt and pepper. Add the butter and stir until incorporated. Divide the mussels among 4 shallow bowls and serve.

I was fortunate to be in Venice one year on November 21 for the Festa della Salute, during which thousands of Venetians, and some tourists, visit the Salute Church to celebrate the strong tie between the city and the Virgin Mary. Fresh sardines are traditional during this particular festival. When I tried the stuffed sardines at a little restaurant near the church, I thought they were so enchanting and tasty, I came up with these sardine "sandwiches." If you like fresh sardines, you will love these. They're a delicious little starter.

venetian-style stuffed sardines | *serves 4*

8 fresh sardines
3 tablespoons chopped fresh flat-leaf parsley
2 tablespoons fresh or dried bread crumbs
2 tablespoons olive oil, plus more for drizzling
1 small yellow onion, thinly sliced
1 fennel bulb, thinly sliced
1 tablespoon pine nuts
1 garlic clove, minced
Kosher salt and freshly ground black pepper
2 tablespoons fresh lemon juice, plus 1^1/2 teaspoons grated zest
Extra virgin olive oil
4 lemon wedges

1. Slit the sardines from end to end without cutting all the way through. Clean the fish and remove any bones. Rinse well. Dry the sardines with paper towels, transfer to a plate or container, cover, and refrigerate until needed.
2. Preheat the oven to 400°F.
3. In a small bowl, mix 1 tablespoon of the parsley with 1 tablespoon of the bread crumbs and set aside.
4. In a saucepan set over medium heat, heat the olive oil. When hot, add the onion, fennel, and pine nuts and cook, stirring, for 2 to 3 minutes, or until the pine nuts are lightly browned.
5. Add the garlic and remaining bread crumbs to the saucepan and cook for about 2 minutes, or until the crumbs begin to crisp slightly. Add 1 tablespoon of the remaining parsley and season to taste with salt and pepper. (If using within an hour, set aside at room temperature. Otherwise, cover and refrigerate for up to 24 hours. Let the filling return to room temperature before using.)

6.   Lightly oil a casserole dish just large enough to easily hold 4 of the butterflied sardines in a single layer without touching each other. Arrange 4 sardines in the dish, skin sides down. Season with salt and pepper. Spoon the filling over the fish and spread it over the meaty parts. Top with the remaining sardines, skin sides up. Position the sardines tail to tail so they sandwich the filling. Sprinkle the reserved parsley–bread crumb mixture over the sardines. Drizzle with olive oil and about a tablespoon of the lemon juice and bake for about 10 minutes, depending on the size of the sardines, until cooked through and the filling is hot. If the filling is still warm when you lay it on the fish, the cooking time will be about 8 minutes.

7.   Put 2 sardines (1 "sandwich") on each of 4 plates. Serve hot or at room temperature, drizzled with the remaining lemon juice and extra virgin olive oil. Garnish with the zest, remaining tablespoon of parsley, and lemon wedges.

My parents referred to cardoons as "Depression food" because they grew so prolifically in our back garden without much help—the kind of vegetable that is always available, even in very hard times. Although the Depression was long over by my childhood, we were one of the few families that still ate them. Cardoons are commonly eaten in Italy and even considered something of a delicacy, despite their easy cultivation, but Americans are not very familiar with them. These close cousins to the artichoke resemble large celery. Gloria Tramonto, my mom, cooked them with cheese, tomato sauce, and butter. Very tasty! I have refined my mom's dish a little for a hearty and very Italian antipasti that will start off any meal with reassuring flavors and textures.

cardoons al forno | *serves 4*

3 lemons, halved

2 pounds cardoons

2 tablespoons kosher salt, plus more for seasoning

All-purpose flour, for dredging

2 large eggs, beaten

$1/2$ cup olive oil

Cracked black pepper

3 cups Tomato Sauce (page 167)

1 cup shredded fresh mozzarella cheese

$3/4$ cup freshly grated Parmigiano-Reggiano cheese

2 tablespoons unsalted butter

2 tablespoons torn fresh basil

1. Fill a bowl with cold water mixed with the juice of 1 lemon. Trim the cardoons and scrape off their outer skin, as you would a carrot. Cut into $3/4$-inch lengths and drop into the water.

2. In a large stockpot, bring about 6 quarts of water to a boil. Lift the cardoons from the acidulated water and drop into the boiling water. Add the salt and the juice from the other 2 lemons. Bring the water back to a boil over medium-high heat and cook for about 30 minutes, until tender but not fully cooked. Lift the cardoons from the water and drain on paper towels.

3. Preheat the oven to 350°F.

4. Spread the flour on one shallow dish and put the eggs in another. Dredge the cardoons first in flour and then dip them in the eggs.

5. Meanwhile, heat the olive oil in a large sauté pan over high heat until hot but not smoking. Fry the cardoons for 6 to 8 minutes, or until golden brown. Fry them in batches, taking care not to overcrowd the pan. Drain on a plate lined with paper towels. Season with salt and pepper. When all are cooked, transfer the cardoons to a casserole dish large enough to hold them in several layers.

6. In a saucepan, heat the tomato sauce over medium-high heat until bubbling. Pour the sauce over the cardoons and top with the mozzarella and Parmesan. Dot the casserole with the butter and bake for 15 to 20 minutes, until the cardoons are bubbling hot and tender.

7. Divide the cardoons among 4 plates and garnish with basil.

White beans with tomato is a staple in all Italian households, and the Tramonto house was no exception when I was growing up. Both my grandmothers made it as a side dish for pork chops or veal, but now I like to serve it as an antipasti. I let it cool to room temperature and it's just wonderful: slightly sophisticated, drizzled with really good olive oil, and yet homey at the same time.

white beans with stewed tomatoes | *serves 4*

1 pound cannellini beans
2 sprigs fresh thyme
2 fresh sage leaves
1 sprig fresh rosemary
1 bay leaf
$^1/_2$ cup olive oil
$^1/_2$ pound bacon, cut into $^1/_4$ inch dice (preferably slab bacon)
1 cup diced Spanish onion
1 tablespoon minced garlic
1 teaspoon crushed red pepper flakes
1 cup diced celery
1 cup diced carrot
1 cup diced fennel
5 ounces Parmigiano-Reggiano cheese rind or chunk of cheese,
     plus 2 tablespoons grated
6 cups chicken stock
One 14-ounce can crushed tomatoes
2 tablespoons sherry vinegar
Kosher salt and cracked black pepper
1 tablespoon chopped fresh flat-leaf parsley
1 tablespoon chopped fresh basil
2 tablespoons extra virgin olive oil

1. Put the beans in a large bowl or pot with enough cold water to cover. Set aside to soak at room temperature for at least 8 hours. Change the water once or twice, if possible. Drain.
2. Wrap the thyme, sage, rosemary, and bay leaf in cheesecloth and, using a piece of kitchen twine, tie into a bundle to make a bouquet garni. Set aside. *(continued)*

1. *To make the ragu:* Put the mushrooms in a small bowl and pour the wine over them. Set aside to soak and hydrate for 20 to 30 minutes. Drain, reserving both the mushrooms and the wine. Strain the wine through a fine-mesh sieve or chinois.

2. In a large, heavy saucepan, heat the olive oil over medium-high heat. Add the sausage and cook, breaking it into pieces with a wooden spoon, for about 5 minutes, until lightly browned and much of the fat is rendered. Using a slotted spoon, lift the sausage from the pan and set aside. Add the pork and beef to the fat in the pan and cook for about 10 minutes, until browned. Season with salt and pepper. Using a slotted spoon, lift the meat from the pan and add it to the sausage. Leave the fat in the pan.

3. Add the onions and garlic to the pan and sauté for 2 to 3 minutes, or until lightly browned. Add the reserved wine, bring to a boil, reduce the heat, and simmer briskly for about 3 minutes or until reduced by half.

4. Return the meat to the pan, season again with salt and pepper, and add the stock, tomatoes, basil, oregano, fennel, bay leaf, and reserved mushrooms. Simmer gently for approximately 1 hour, or until the meat is tender. Skim any fat that rises to the top of the pan during cooking. Cover to keep warm and set aside.

5. *To make the polenta:* Put the stock and the cream in a saucepan over medium-high heat and bring to a boil. Slowly pour the polenta into the hot liquid, whisking briskly to prevent clumping. Reduce the heat to low and cook, whisking constantly, for about 10 minutes, or until the liquid is absorbed.

6. Add the cheese and butter, stirring gently until incorporated.

7. Spoon a mound of soft polenta on each of 4 or 6 plates or shallow bowls. Ladle the ragu over the polenta and garnish with basil, parsley, and grated Parmesan.

Chef Chris Pandel, a good friend, my chef de cuisine, and someone who helped me immensely with this book, came up with this recipe during the holidays when we were working together on the seasonal menu. If this isn't the perfect antipasto, or first course, for Thanksgiving (or any time during the fall and winter), I don't know what would be! The deep-fried parsnips are absolutely delicious, and when topped with wine-soaked cranberries, the flavors and textures are at once unexpected and familiar. As I said earlier in the book, don't be afraid of deep-frying. Let the oil get hot enough and allow it to regain its temperature between batches, and you will do fine. And everyone will be glad you decided to undertake the task. Thanks, Chris!

parsnips with cinnamon cranberries | *serves 4*

1 cup Marsala wine
Grated zest and juice of 1 orange
$^1/2$ teaspoon ground cinnamon
$^3/4$ cup dried cranberries
3 quarts peanut oil, for frying
2 pounds parsnips
2 tablespoons extra virgin olive oil
Kosher salt and cracked black pepper
1 tablespoon julienned fresh mint

1. In a small saucepan, warm the Marsala. Do not let it boil, or the alcohol will boil away. Remove the pan from the heat and add the orange zest, juice, and cinnamon.

2. Put the cranberries in a nonreactive bowl and pour the warm wine over them. Set aside for 1 hour to macerate so the cranberries hydrate.

3. Meanwhile, in a large, heavy pot, heat the oil to 250°F over high heat. Use a deep-frying thermometer to determine the oil's temperature; then moderate the heat to maintain the temperature. You can also tell if the oil is hot enough if it bubbles slightly when something (such as a piece of bread or the handle of a wooden spoon) is submerged in it.

4. Rinse the parsnips and then let them dry completely or wipe them dry with paper towels. Put the whole parsnips in the oil, with the skin and top still attached. Fry for 7 to 10 minutes or until fully tender inside and lightly browned outside. Lift from the oil and set aside to drain on paper towels. When cool enough, cut each one lengthwise into 4 pieces.

5. To serve, divide the parsnip quarters among 4 plates, drizzle with olive oil, and season to taste with salt and pepper. Spoon cranberries and juice around the parsnips and garnish with mint.

I came to this little antipasto in a roundabout way, with the first stop being the Alsace region of France. The food there is fantastic and is influenced by bordering Germany and Switzerland. I had a fabulous dish made with red cabbage and bacon, and so, in Tramonto style, immediately decided to make it Italian, primarily by using pancetta instead of bacon. The dish's second stop was as an accompaniment for chicken, but it got so many rave reviews from my customers, I quickly decided to let it stand on its own as a starter. So here it is at the third stop, as an antipasto. It has found its home.

braised red cabbage with pancetta | *serves 4*

^{1}/3 cup olive oil

1 cup diced pancetta

1 cup diced red onion

1 tablespoon minced garlic

1 medium head red cabbage, julienned and rinsed in cold water

2 oranges, quartered

2 cups red wine

^{1}/2 cup red wine vinegar

2 tablespoons brown sugar

2 tablespoons unsalted butter

1 tablespoon honey

1 teaspoon freshly grated nutmeg

Kosher salt and cracked black pepper

1 tablespoon chopped fresh tarragon

1 tablespoon chopped fresh flat-leaf parsley

1. In a large sauté pan, heat the olive oil over medium heat. When hot, add the pancetta and cook until crispy. Add the onion and garlic and sauté for 2 to 3 minutes, or until the onion is translucent. Stir in the cabbage.
2. Squeeze the juice from the orange quarters into the pan and then drop the quarters into the pan, too. Sauté for about 3 minutes.
3. Add the red wine and vinegar, lower the heat to medium-low, cover tightly, and cook very slowly for 15 to 20 minutes, until the liquid is nearly gone and the cabbage is bright purple.
4. Add the brown sugar, butter, honey, and nutmeg, stirring to melt the butter and sugar. Season to taste with salt and pepper. Just before serving, stir in the tarragon and parsley.
5. Divide the cabbage among 4 plates and serve warm.

When I traveled in Sicily, I was served several versions of roasted cauliflower with golden raisins. I was invited to dinner in a private home and served a similar dish as an antipasto, and knew I had to recreate it at home. So, here it is, and is it good! Even if you think you don't like cauliflower, you will love this preparation, and it will become one of your staple antipasti.

cauliflower with golden raisins and lemon-garlic bread crumbs | *serves 4*

1 cup golden raisins
1 cup orange juice
5 to 6 cups cauliflower florets, about 1^1/2 inches in diameter
^{1}/3 cup extra virgin olive oil
^{1}/2 cup thinly sliced red onion
2 tablespoons fresh lemon juice
2 garlic cloves, thinly sliced
Kosher salt and cracked black pepper
^{1}/2 cup drained capers
2 tablespoons freshly grated Parmigiano-Reggiano cheese
1 cup Lemon-Garlic Bread Crumbs (page 71)
2 tablespoons chopped fresh flat-leaf parsley

1. Preheat the oven to 450°F.
2. In a small bowl, soak the raisins in the orange juice for about 20 minutes, until plumped. Drain and discard the juice.
3. Meanwhile, fill a large pot about halfway with lightly salted water and bring to a boil over medium-high heat. Add the cauliflower and blanch for about 2 minutes, or until they begin to soften and are about half-cooked. Drain.
4. Put the florets in a large ovenproof sauté pan or roasting pan. Drizzle with olive oil and sprinkle with the onion, lemon juice, and garlic. Season with salt and pepper.
5. Cook on top of the stove over medium heat for 3 to 4 minutes, stirring to heat evenly. Transfer the pan to the oven and roast for about 10 minutes, stirring occasionally to ensure even roasting. Take the pan from the oven and sprinkle with the capers, cheese, and drained raisins. Top with the bread crumbs and roast for 5 to 7 minutes, until lightly browned and crusty.
6. Spoon the cauliflower on a serving platter, garnish with parsley, and serve warm.

These substantial antipasti, called Suppli alla Romana in Italy, are crowd-pleasers, big and small, because they embody a few surefire elements: oozing cheese, a light tomato sauce, well-seasoned meat, saltiness, and a little crunch from the crispy, fried balls. I first had a rice ball in Barcelona, Spain, at a tapas bar, where the rice was stuffed with a mixture of ham and cheese. I noted as much in my trusty travel journal and later translated the concept into a very Italian antipasto. Since then, I have tasted similar rice balls throughout Italy. *Fantastico!*

stuffed rice balls | *serves 4*

2 cups beef stock

1^2/3 cups chopped ripe plum tomatoes

4 tablespoons (^{1}/2 stick) unsalted butter

1^2/3 cup uncooked Arborio rice

2 large eggs, beaten

^{2}/3 cup freshly grated Parmigiano-Reggiano cheese

2 ounces prosciutto, chopped

1 yellow onion, chopped

1 tablespoon minced garlic

7 ounces lean ground beef

2 tablespoons tomato paste

^{1}/4 cup chicken stock or water

Kosher salt and cracked black pepper

5 ounces mozzarella or provolone cheese, diced

^{3}/4 cup fresh or dried bread crumbs

Canola oil, for frying

1 tablespoon chopped fresh flat-leaf parsley

1. In a saucepan, combine the beef stock, tomatoes, and 3 tablespoons of the butter and bring to a boil over medium-high heat. Stir in the rice, cover tightly, and simmer for about 20 minutes, stirring occasionally, until the rice is done. Transfer to a bowl.

2. Stir the eggs and Parmesan into the hot rice. Set aside to cool.

3. In a skillet, melt the remaining 1 tablespoon of butter over medium heat. Add the prosciutto, onion, and garlic and sauté for 2 to 3 minutes, or until the onion softens. Add the beef and cook for 3 to 4 minutes longer, breaking up the meat as it cooks, until browned. Drain the fat from the pan.

4.   Stir together the chicken stock and tomato paste until smooth. Add to the pan, season to taste with salt and pepper, and bring to a simmer over medium heat. Cook for 8 to 10 minutes, or until the meat is cooked through.

5.   With a spoon, scoop out egg-shaped portions of the rice and press on the center of each one to make an indentation. Spoon about 1 teaspoon of the meat mixture into each indentation and top with a few pieces of cheese. Using your fingers, push the rice up and around the filling. You should make about 24 balls.

6.   Spread the bread crumbs on a shallow plate and roll each rice ball in the crumbs to coat.

7.   In a deep, heavy pot, add enough oil to cover the balls when they are fried. Bring to a boil over high heat.

8.   Using a slotted spoon, submerge the rice balls in the hot oil and fry for 3 to 5 minutes, or until golden brown. Do not crowd the pan. Remove with a slotted spoon and drain on a plate lined with paper towels.

9.   Line a serving bowl with wax paper or paper napkins. Fill the bowl with rice balls and garnish with chopped parsley. Serve warm. If necessary, rewarm the rice ball in a low oven.

cheese

the cheese course

Praise

God for cheese! I can't imagine a
world without all kinds of cheeses—firm and
flaky, smooth and creamy, dry, crumbly, or oozing. They're
all good. I have never had a restaurant that did not serve a cheese
course, and never will. By the same token, I couldn't write this book
without a chapter devoted exclusively to gorgeous Italian cheeses. The recipes
here showcase the cheeses themselves so they are the focus of the dish, not an accent
or flavoring. Italy's cheesemaking tradition is long and proud, but it tends to celebrate the
home rather than the *haute*. The cheeses of Italy are more modest than some of France's
contributions, but they are no less noble. Arguably the most noble of all is Parmigiano-
Reggiano, the dry yet moist grating cheese that the Western world has adopted as its own. But
Italian cheeses don't begin and end with Parm; they include glories such as Gorgonzola, Fontina,
pecorino, and Taleggio. All magnificent when you seek out the best.
When searching for the right cheese, don't overlook similar styles that may not be imported from
Italy. American artisanal cheesemakers are among the best in the world and have looked to Europe
for ideas and inspiration. The American cheesemaking revolution is nothing short of miraculous.
In this chapter, I pair Italian beauties with sweet, salty, and acidic foods to offset the creamy,
buttery, tangy, fruity, mellow, sharp, and salty qualities of the cheeses. And I can think of no
better way to bring these good flavors and textures home than with a great bottle of Italian
wine. Set these little plates out the next time friends drop by, or plan a gathering where the
cheese and wine hold center stage. *Salut!*

ABOUT THE WINE

*Italy's sweet and sticky wine roster leaves nothing to be desired: fizzy white Moscato
d'Asti and fizzy red Brachetto from Piedmont; unctuous Van Santo, Passion,
and Amiable made from many grapes in almost all of Italy's wine-
producing regions. So, never fear the Italian cheese course;
options abound!*

If you can find fresh ricotta, carefully made by a good cheesemaker, you will discover a product totally different from what is mass-produced for supermarket consumption. Match the creamy, mildly sweet, moist cheese with persimmons and the result is outrageous. No persimmons? Try it with peaches, pears, or apricots. Equally praiseworthy! When I was young, my grandparents kept fresh ricotta in the house at all times and used it as other cooks might use sour cream. Ricotta on top of pancakes, pasta, baked potatoes, and toast with jam. They sweetened it when needed, and salted it at other times.

Ricotta was developed to make good use of whey, a by-product of cheesemaking. The word means "recooked" and refers to the process of heating the whey so that it creates curds. The drained curds become ricotta. According to cheese expert Steven Jenkins, whom I greatly admire, ricotta has only been made for the past one hundred years or so. Good luck for us! Italian ricotta is most often made from sheep's or goat's milk whey, although it can be made from the whey of water buffalo's or cow's milk. In the United States, it's made almost exclusively from cow's milk and tends to be a little moister and sweeter.

format di ricotta with vanilla-poached persimmon | *serves 4*

4 ripe, firm Fuyu persimmons (see Note)
$^3/_4$ cup freshly squeezed orange juice, strained
$^1/_2$ cup dry white wine
$^1/_4$ cup sugar
$^1/_2$ vanilla bean, split (see Note)
1 teaspoon minced fresh ginger
$^1/_4$ teaspoon ground cinnamon
$^1/_2$ pound fresh Italian ricotta cheese
2 tablespoons julienned mint
8 whole wheat crackers

1. Stem, peel, and seed the persimmons. Cut each one into 8 wedges.
2. In a saucepan, mix the orange juice, wine, sugar, vanilla bean, ginger, and cinnamon. Add the persimmon wedges and bring to a boil over medium-high heat. Reduce the heat, cover, and simmer for 14 to 16 minutes, or until the persimmons are tender. Adjust the heat to maintain

the simmer. Using a slotted spoon, transfer the persimmons to a bowl, leaving the syrup in the saucepan.

3. Bring the syrup to a boil over medium-high heat and cook at a gentle boil for 4 to 5 minutes, or until reduced by half. Discard the vanilla bean and set the syrup aside, covered to keep warm.

4. Cut the ricotta cheese into four equal pieces and put each on a plate. Arrange 6 to 8 persimmon wedges next to the cheese. Drizzle the syrup over the persimmons and garnish each plate with mint. Serve with whole wheat crackers.

NOTE Fuyu persimmons are smaller and rounder than Hachiya persimmons, the other variety most available in the United States. Fuyu persimmons also have a lighter color and, when ripe, are firm and crisp with a lovely sweet flavor. They can be eaten out of hand, broiled briefly, or simmered in liquid, as I do here. In much of the world, persimmons are known as *kaki*.

I split fresh whole vanilla beans lengthwise and then scrape the seeds from one side, usually with the back of a small spoon. I take the other half and bury it in sugar to preserve it until needed. It perfumes the sugar with tantalizing flavor and keeps for a couple of months. (I can rarely wait that long!) Otherwise, wrap the split bean in plastic and refrigerate it for up to 3 weeks.

Umbriaco cheese is soaked in red wine, to the point that the rind turns purple and the cheese tastes ever so slightly of grapes. Similar to Asiago, which is one of Italy's most popular and versatile cheeses, I like the depth and interest of the Umbriaco. The word translates to "drunkard" or "inebriated," and that small fact alone makes the cheese fun to eat and to serve! Don't hesitate to use Asiago cheese instead, if it's easier to find. Both cheeses taste good alongside the crisp fennel salad and make a *fantastico* cheese course.

umbriaco al vino rosa cheese with shaved fennel salad | *serves 4*

1 cup trimmed, cored, and thinly shaved fennel,
    plus 1 tablespoon chopped fronds
3 tablespoons extra virgin olive oil
Juice of 1 lemon
1 tablespoon torn fresh basil
3 grindings of black pepper
Kosher salt
$1/2$ pound Umbriaco al Vino Rosa cheese
4 thick slices sourdough bread, toasted

1. In a small bowl, mix the shaved fennel and fennel fronds, olive oil, lemon juice, basil, and pepper. Season to taste with salt.
2. Cut the cheese into four equal pieces and put each on a plate. Spoon the fennel salad next to the cheese and serve with toast.

Pecorino cheeses are crafted throughout much of Italy. My all-time favorites are the pecorinos made in Tuscany, particularly the cheeses from near the town of Pienza. *Pecora* is the Italian word for sheep, and these sheep's-milk cheeses have a lovely yet intense flavor with a mildly peppery finish when aged for about six months. Terrific for snacking (cube it and store it covered with fruity olive oil), adding to salads, or tossing with pasta, it can be cut into pieces and topped with homemade apricot jam for a savory dessert.

pecorino toscano with apricot jam | *serves 4*

$3^1/2$ to 4 pounds ripe apricots, peaches, or plums

3 cups sugar

$1/4$ cup fresh lemon juice

$1/2$ vanilla bean, split

$3/4$ cup stemmed and torn watercress

1 tablespoon saba vinegar or aged balsamic vinegar (see Note, page 39)

Extra virgin olive oil

Kosher salt and cracked black pepper

$1/2$ pound pecorino Toscano cheese

Four $1/4$-inch baguette, toasted and brushed with extra virgin olive oil

1. Wash, peel, and pit the apricots. Hold them over a large saucepan and crush by hand, dropping the crushed fruit into the pan.

2. Set the pan over high heat and, stirring constantly, add the sugar, lemon juice, and vanilla bean until well combined and boiling. Boil for 30 minutes, skimming off and discarding any foam that rises to the surface.

3. Pour the hot jam into two to three 3-ounce sterilized canning jars. Put the canning lids on the jars and screw in place with the rings. Set aside to cool. Refrigerate for up to 1 month.

4. In a mixing bowl, toss the watercress with the vinegar. Drizzle with a little olive oil, toss again, and season to taste with salt and pepper.

5. Cut the cheese into four equal pieces and put each on a plate. Spoon some watercress salad on each plate and garnish with 1 tablespoon of the apricot jam. Serve with toasted baguette.

NOTE To sterilize the jars, submerge them in boiling water for 15 minutes. Remove the pot from the heat and leave the jars in the hot water until ready to use. Sterilize the rubber rings and screw-on tops in the same way but in another pot.

You may not have heard of Scamorza, but it's an ancient cheese from water buffalo's or cow's milk, still made in the time-honored way in Lombardy. It resembles mozzarella, but differs in that it's denser, chewier, and drier with a salty mildness. Those qualities make it the perfect accent to the sweet acid of orange and the pepperiness of arugula. For a delicious change of pace, warm up the cheese just until it begins to melt, then lay it over the salad. Scamorza is equally alluring with nothing more than a grind of the peppermill and a drizzle of green, fruity extra virgin olive oil. *Fantastico!*

scamorza with arugula and oranges | *serves 4*

2 seasonal oranges, the best available, such as Florida Honey,
    blood oranges, Valencia, or Nazelina
1 cup arugula
1 tablespoon torn fresh basil
1 tablespoon extra virgin olive oil
$^1/_2$ pound Scamorza cheese
4 thick slices raisin-nut bread, toasted

1. Peel 1 of the oranges and, holding it over a bowl to catch the juices, separate it into sections. Drop the sections into the bowl along with the juices. Add the arugula, basil, and olive oil.
2. Juice the second orange and add the juice to the salad. Toss well.
3. Cut the cheese into thin slices and divide them among 4 plates. Spoon equal amounts of the salad on each plate next to the cheese. Serve with a slice of toast.

I visited the Lago Monate cheesemakers one year with my good friend Larry Binstein from European Imports. The centuries-old company is near Lake Como, and as we toured the aging rooms and tasted the cheeses, my appreciation for this monumental cheese increased. I am not surprised, since I've read that the ancient Romans loved Taleggio cheese—I am sure as much as I do! A well-made Taleggio sets your taste buds singing with its mild nuttiness, sweet overtones, whisper of salty and sour undertones, and boast of butteriness. Wow! Like French Brie, the cow's-milk cheese oozes as it warms up, so I can't imagine a better pairing for the quince paste. Plus, it makes perfect sense to match Taleggio with quince, because the Romans also prized the fragrant, old-fashioned fruit. Quinces resemble malformed yellow apples and are easier than ever to find; I have seen them in supermarkets in the fall. I garnish this with lightly oiled and salted Marcona almonds, which complement the sweetness of the fruit and the cheese. If you can't find them, use any almonds or lightly toasted pecans.

taleggio with quince paste and
marcona almonds | *serves 4*

2 pounds quinces
About 3 cups sugar
Grated zest of 1 lemon
$^1/_4$ teaspoon ground cinnamon
$^1/_2$ pound Taleggio cheese
24 Marcona almonds
8 sesame crackers or four $^1/_4$-inch slices baguette, toasted
    and brushed with extra virgin olive oil

1. Without peeling them, cut the quinces lengthwise into eighths and remove the cores. Put in a large saucepan with $^1/_2$ cup water. Bring to a simmer over medium-high heat. Cover and simmer for 30 to 40 minutes, until the fruit is soft. Adjust the heat to maintain the simmer.

2. Using a food mill or fine-mesh sieve, puree the fruit. Measure the fruit in cups and then return it to the saucepan. Add the same measure of sugar that you have of quince. Bring to a simmer over medium heat, stirring constantly, until the puree is very thick and pulls away from the sides of the pan. Fold in the lemon zest and cinnamon.

3. Spread or press the quince mixture into the bottom of a pan or flat plate large enough to contain it in a $^1/_2$-inch-thick layer. Set aside, uncovered, to dry for at least 8 hours.

4. Cut the paste into wedges and turn the wedges upside down. Let them dry for another 5 to 6 hours.

5. Cut the Taleggio into $^1/_4$-inch-thick wedges and discard the rind. Divide the cheese wedges among the 4 plates, arranging them on one side of the plate. Cut the quince wedges into smaller wedges, rectangles, or any desired shape and set them on the other side of the plate. Garnish with almonds and serve with crackers.

I rely on Gorgonzola dolce throughout the book partly because it is so versatile, but primarily because I absolutely love the mild, sweet, creamy blue cheese. Anyone with a fondness for blue cheese will gravitate to this lovely cheese, and even those who are not major fans of blues may fall for this in a big way! My grandparents kept a cheese plate around most of the time, and more often than not the two offerings were Gorgonzola dolce and Parmigiano-Reggiano. I never thought of either as anything special, although I now respect the years of knowledge that go into the making of each. Dolce is made in Lombardy near the town of Gorgonzola and aged according to DOC regulations. I pair it here with pears and spiced walnuts, reminiscent of the classic pear, walnut, and Gorgonzola cheese salad—just deconstructed so the cheese is the focus. If you have a perfectly ripe pear, no need to roast it.

gorgonzola dolce with roasted pears and spiced walnuts | *serves 4*

$^1/_4$ cup white wine

Juice of $^1/_2$ orange

2 tablespoons honey

$1^1/_2$ tablespoons unsalted butter, cut into small pieces

$^1/_2$ vanilla bean, split

1 cinnamon stick

$^1/_4$ teaspoon cracked black pepper

2 large, firm, ripe pears, such as Bosc or Anjou, peeled, cored, and halved

Juice of $^1/_2$ lemon

$^1/_2$ pound Gorgonzola dolce, at room temperature, cut into 4 pieces (see page 36)

$^1/_4$ cup chopped Spiced Walnuts (page 252)

1. Preheat the oven to 400°F.
2. In a shallow baking dish that will hold the pear halves in one layer, combine the wine, orange juice, honey, butter, vanilla bean, cinnamon stick, and pepper. Mix thoroughly.
3. Rub each pear half with lemon juice to prevent browning and put them, cut sides down, in the baking dish. Spoon some of the wine-orange mixture over each pear and cover the dish with parchment paper.
4. Bake for 20 to 30 minutes, until the pears are tender when pierced with a small, sharp knife.

(continued)

Do not overcook or they will fall apart. Carefully transfer the pears to a plate or cutting board and let them cool to room temperature.

5. Meanwhile, pour the baking juices into a small saucepan and bring to a boil over medium-high heat. Cook until reduced to $^1/_4$ cup or the consistency of a light syrup. Discard the vanilla bean and cinnamon stick.

6. Slice each pear half lengthwise into 6 slices. Place each pear half on a plate, fanning the slices slightly. Spoon 1 tablespoon of the warm syrup over each pear half and set a piece of Gorgonzola next to each one. Sprinkle the walnuts over the pears and serve.

spiced walnuts | makes about 1 cup

1 tablespoon packed light brown sugar
2 teaspoons walnut oil
$^1/_4$ teaspoon cayenne
$^1/_4$ teaspoon ground cumin
1 cup walnut halves

1. Preheat the oven to 350°F.

2. In a mixing bowl, stir the sugar, oil, cayenne, and cumin until well mixed. Add the walnuts and toss until thoroughly coated.

3. Spread the walnuts on a baking sheet in a single layer and bake for 15 to 20 minutes, until fragrant and slightly darker in color. Stir them at least once to promote even cooking, and take care they do not burn. Let the walnuts cool and then chop them coarsely.

4. The spiced nuts can be stored in a airtight container for up to 2 days.

As I explained in the recipe for Fonduta on page 79, Fontina Val D'Aosta has been produced in a valley near the Swiss border in the northwest part of Italy since the Middle Ages. The cows that produce the milk for this famed cheese graze in alpine pastures on green, green grass sprinkled with flowers. The resulting cheese is firm yet easy to slice, eminently meltable, buttery and nutty with just a hint of honey—all of which make it just a little sweeter than other fontinas and rather similar to Gruyère. I caution that you pay close attention when buying fontina. Many that are not made in the DOC-designated region of Italy are still very good, but there are enough poor examples bearing the name that it pays to buy with care. And when the fontina is high quality, it rises to the occasion. It goes very well with the crisp, tart green apples and picks up the flavor of the honey in this small cheese plate.

fontina val d'aosta with green apple salad and chestnut honey | *serves 4*

2 green apples, such as Granny Smith, peeled, cored, and julienned

1 tablespoon julienned fresh mint

1 tablespoon fresh lemon juice

Kosher salt and cracked black pepper

$^1/2$ pound Fontina Val d'Aosta cheese

$^1/4$ cup chestnut honey or other mild honey

4 thick slices multigrain bread, toasted

1. In a mixing bowl, toss the apples, mint, and lemon juice. Season to taste with salt and pepper.
2. Cut the cheese into four equal pieces and put each on a plate. Spoon about $^1/2$ cup of the apple salad next to each piece of cheese. Drizzle the honey over the salad and serve with a slice of toast.

This cheese course is one I frequently serve to guests at home, and every time it's enthusiastically received. Asiago is a little softer than aged Parm, with a nutty, sweet flavor that is gorgeous with glazed onions. I also find it's a *fantastico* red wine cheese, and goes quite nicely with a dessert Sauternes.

asiago cheese with glazed cipolline onions | *serves 4*

$1^1/2$ pounds cippoline onions, skins on (see Note)
$^3/4$ cup dry sherry
$^1/3$ cup raisins
3 tablespoons honey
$1^1/2$ tablespoons unsalted butter
Juice of 1 orange
1 teaspoon chopped fresh thyme
Kosher salt and cracked black pepper
1 tablespoon sherry vinegar
$^1/2$ pound Asiago cheese
Four $^1/4$-inch slices baguette, toasted and brushed with extra virgin olive oil

1. Bring a large saucepan of lightly salted water to a boil. Cook the onions, with their skins, over high heat for 2 to 3 minutes, just until they begin to soften. Drain and set aside to cool. When cool enough to handle, slice off the root ends and remove the papery onion skin; leave whole.

2. In a sauté pan, mix the sherry, raisins, honey, 3 tablespoons water, the butter, orange juice, and thyme. Add the onions and bring to a simmer over medium-high heat. Reduce the heat to maintain a simmer, cover, and cook for 15 to 20 minutes, until the onions are tender when pierced with a small sharp knife. Adjust the heat as needed to maintain the simmer.

3. Remove the cover, season to taste with salt and pepper, and simmer for 2 to 4 minutes longer, or until the sauce reduces almost to a glaze. Stir the onions occasionally so they color evenly. Remove from the heat and let the onions cool slightly in the pan. Stir in the vinegar and set aside to cool to room temperature.

4. Cut the cheese into four equal pieces and put each on a plate. Mound the onions next to the cheese. Serve with a baguette slice.

You don't have to travel to Italy—or even an Italian specialty food store—for good goat cheese. American cheesemakers, such as Judy Shad of Cowgirl Creamery in Greenville, Indiana; Susi Cahn from Coach Farm in New York's Hudson Valley; and Laura Chenel from the Sonoma, California, cheese company that bears her name, produce outstanding cheeses that home cooks and chefs alike enjoy. But Caprino Noce is a goat cheese close to my heart, in part because I fondly recall spending a lovely afternoon on the veranda of a winery in the Piedmont, drinking a glass of big, Italian red wine and eating this cheese, which comes wrapped in walnut leaves. The walnut leaf adds just enough nutty flavor to make a subtle but real difference. My friend Max McCalman, who has written some wonderful books on cheese, reminds us that Italian goat cheeses are "worthy of investigation." I couldn't agree more. I have stopped at small goat cheese farms throughout Italy, meeting the cheesemakers and tasting cheeses from the very fresh to slightly aged specimens that are covered with ash or herbs, or wrapped in leaves.

goat cheese with frisée salad and extra virgin olive oil | *serves 4*

1 tablespoon apple cider vinegar
1 tablespoon chopped fresh chives
1 teaspoon chopped fresh tarragon
1 teaspoon honey
$^1/_2$ teaspoon fresh lemon juice
2 tablespoons extra virgin olive oil, plus more for drizzling
Kosher salt and cracked black pepper
1 cup stemmed frisée
2 ripe plums, peeled, cored, and thinly sliced
$^1/_2$ pound slightly aged goat cheese
Four $^1/_4$-inch slices baguette, toasted and brushed with extra virgin olive oil, optional

1. In a mixing bowl, whisk together the vinegar, chives, tarragon, honey, and lemon juice. Slowly whisk in the olive oil and when incorporated, season to taste with salt and pepper. Add the frisée and sliced plums and toss gently to coat with the dressing.
2. Cut the cheese into four equal pieces and put each on a plate. Drizzle olive oil over the cheese and season with pepper. Mound a quarter of the frisée salad next to the cheese on each plate. Serve with a baguette slice.

SOURCES

Hard-to-Find Ingredients and Equipment

Following are sources I use in my restaurants for food and equipment. If there is something you cannot find from local purveyors, one of these merchants may well be able to help you.

Seafood and Fish

Browne Trading
260 Commercial Street; Stop 3
Portland, ME 04101
Phone: 207–766–2402
Fax: 207–766–2404
www.brownetrading.com
All fish

Steve Connolly Seafood Company
34 Newmarket Square
Boston, MA 02118
Phone: 800–225–5595
www.steveconnollyseafood.com
Lobsters; shellfish

M. F. Foley Fish Company
24 West Howell Street
Dorchester, MA 02125
Phone: 800–225–9995
Fax: 617–288–1300
foleyfish.com
All fish

Fortune Fish
2442 North 77th Street
Elmwood Park, IL 60707
Phone: 630–860–7100
www.fortunefishco.net
All fish

Honolulu Fish
1907 Democrat Street
Honolulu, HI 96819
Phone: 808–833–1123
Fax: 888–475–6244
www.honolulufish.com
All fish

Pierless Fish
Brooklyn Navy Yard
Brooklyn, NY 11205
Phone: 718–222–4441
www.pierlessfish.com
All fish

Plitt Seafood
1445 West Willow Street
Chicago, IL 60061
Phone: 773–276–2200
Fax: 773–276–3350
www.plittcompany.com
All fish

Seafood Merchants
900 Forest Edge Drive
Vernon Hills, IL 60061
Phone: 847–634–0900
Fax: 847–634–1351
www.theseafoodmerchants.com
All fish

Meats, Game, and Poultry

Elysian Fields Farm
Keith Martin
844 Craynes Run Road
Waynesburg, PA 15370
Phone: 724–627–9503
www.elysianfarm.com
Lamb

European Imports
2475 North Elston Avenue
Chicago, IL 60647
Phone: 773–227–0600
Fax: 773–227–6775
www.eiltd.com
All game; wild mushrooms

Jamison Farms
John Jamison
171 Jamison Lane
Latrobe, PA 15650
Phone: 800–237–5262
jamisonfarm.com
Lamb

Millbrook Farms
Phone: 800–774–3337
Fax: 845–677–8457
Venison

Niman Ranch
940 Judson Avenue
Evanston, IL 60202
Phone: 847–570–0200
www.nimanranch.com
Lamb; pork

Stock Yards
340 North Oakley Boulevard
Chicago, IL 60612
Phone: 312–733–6050
Fax: 312–733–0738
www.stockyards.com
All meat

Swan Creek Farms
10531 Wood Road
North Adams, MI 49262
Phone: 517–523–3308
Lamb; pork; eggs; cheese

Produce

Chef's Garden Farms
9009 Huron-Avery Road
Huron, OH 44839
Phone: 800–289–4644
www.chefs-garden.com
All vegetables; herbs

Cornille and Sons
Tom Cornille
2404 S. Wolcott Avenue
Chicago, IL 60608
Phone: 312–226–1015
Fax: 773–847–8482
www.cornilleproduce.com
All vegetables; herbs

Fresh and Wild
2917 Northeast 65th Street
Vancouver, WA 98663
Phone: 360–737–3652
Wild mushrooms

Midwest Foods
3100 West 36th Street
Chicago, IL 60632
Phone:773–927–8870
        800–930–4270
Fax: 773–932–4280
www.mwfoods.com
All vegetables; herbs

Testo Produce
1501 South Blue Island Avenue
Chicago, IL 06008
Phone: 312–226–3237
All produce

Sid Wainer and Son
George Rasmussen
2301 Purchase Street
New Bedford, MA 20746
Phone: 800–423–8333
Fax: 508–999–6795
www.sidwainer.com
Specialty produce; specialty products

Pastry Supplies and Cheeses

Coach Farms
800–999–4628
www.coachfarms.com
Cheeses

Great American Cheese
Giles Schnierle
2320 West 110th Street
Chicago, Il 60643
Phone: 773–779–5055
Fax: 773–779–5227
www.greatamericancheese.com
Cheeses

Neiman Brothers
3322 West Newport Avenue
Chicago, IL 60618
Phone: 773–463–3000
Fax: 773–463–3181
www.neimanbrothers.com
Pastry supplies

Albert Uster Imports, Inc.
911 Gaither Road
Gaithersburg, MD 20877
Phone: 800–231–8154
Fax: 773–761–5412
www.auiswiss.com
Pastry supplies

Equipment

All-Clad Metalcrafters
424 Morganza Road
Canonsburg, PA 15317
Phone: 800–255–2523
Fax: 724–746–5035
www.allclad.com
Smallwares

Chef's Catalog
5950 Colwell Boulevard
Irving, TX 75039
Phone: 800–884–2433
www.chefscatalog.com
Smallwares

Korin
57 Warren Street
New York, NY 10007
Phone: 800–626–2172
212–587–7021
www.korin.com
Knives; Asian china; Asian equipment

Tramonto Cuisine
Chef Rick Tramonto
tramontocuisine@aol.com
Caviar staircases

Viking
111 Front Street
Greenwood, MS 38930
Phone: 662–455–1200
www.vikingrange.com
All equipment

Williams Sonoma
Phone: 877–812–6235
Fax: 702–363–2541
www.williams-sonoma.com
Smallwares

Specialty Products

Anson Mills
1922-C Gervais Street
Columbus, SC 29201
Phone: 803–467–4122
Fax: 803–256–2463
www.ansonmills.com
Stoneground grits

Bukiety Florists
Tony Polega
2000 West Carroll Avenue
Chicago, IL 60612
Phone: 312–733–4580
Flowers

Bragard
215 Park Avenue South
New York, NY 10003
Phone: 212–982–8031
www.bragardusa.com
Chef's clothing

Chefwear
3111 N. Knox Avenue
Chicago, Il 60641
Phone: 800–568–2433
www.chefwear.com
Chef's clothing

European Imports
2475 North Elston Avenue
Chicago, IL 60647
Phone: 773–227–0600
Fax: 773–227–6775
www.eiltd.com
Specialty foods

Illy Coffee
275 Madison Avenue
New York, NY 10016
Phone: 877–469–4559
www.illyusa.com
Coffee

Natural Juice
550 Clayton Court
Wood Dale, IL 60191
Phone: 800–831–6060
Fax: 630–350–2050
www.naturaljuice.com
Fresh juices

Spiceland
6604 West Irving Park Road
Chicago, IL 60634
Phone: 800–352–8671
Fax: 773–736–1217
Spices

Turner Studios
Tim Turner Photography
833 West Chicago Avenue
Chicago, IL 60622
Phone: 312–733–5313
Food photography

Urbani Truffle
380 Meadowbrook Road
Lorin Wales, PA 19454
Phone: 215–699–8780
Fax: 215–699–3859
www.urbanitruffles.com
Truffle products

INDEX

Page numbers in **bold type** indicate photographs.

a

Abruzzi swordfish roll-ups, 215–17, **216**
Ahi tuna, crusted, with pomegranate vinaigrette, 60–62, **61**
Aioli
  black olive, 174; grilled chicken with soppressata salumi and black olive aioli panini, 173–74
  caper, fried smelts with, 203–5, **204**
  lemon, grilled shrimp wrapped in pancetta with, 34–35

roasted garlic, 161; PLT (pancetta, lettuce, and tomato panini) with, 160–61
Al Diauola Osteria, 56
Almond mustard, speck with blood oranges and, 96–97
Almonds
  roasted spaghetti squash with vanilla and Marcona almonds, 210–12, **211**
  Taleggio with quince paste and Marcona almonds, 248–49
Anchovies, 17
  bruschetta with roasted peppers and white anchovies, 116
  marinated white anchovy and dandelion salad, **16**, 17–18
Angel hair frittata with artichokes and black pepper pecorino, 192–93

Anise-orange vinaigrette, 13
  fava and yellow beans with radicchio, goat cheese, and, 12
Antipasti, 191–239
  about, 191
  Abruzzi swordfish roll-ups, 215–17, **216**
  angel hair frittata with artichokes and black pepper pecorino, 192–93
  braised red cabbage with pancetta, 235
  cardoons al forno, 226–27
  cauliflower with golden raisins and lemon-garlic bread crumbs, 236, **237**
  creamy soft polenta with meat ragu, 231–33, **232**
  farro with vegetables, 194–96, **195**

fried smelts with caper aioli, 203–5, **204**

frittata with prosciutto, potato, and spinach, 201–2

green and yellow beans with sherry vinaigrette, 206

grilled baby octopus and fingerling potato salad, 197–200, **198**

Italian sausage with roasted peppers and onions, 220–22, **221**

lobster with garlic and Parmigiano-Reggiano, 213–14

pappa pomodoro, 218, **219**

parsnips with cinnamon cranberries, 234

roasted spaghetti squash with vanilla and Marcona almonds, 210–12, **211**

steamed black mussels with garlic and spicy pepperoni, 223

stuffed rice balls, 238–39

Tuscan panzanella, 207–9, **208**

Venetian-style stuffed sardines, 224–25

white beans with stewed tomatoes, 228–30, **229**

Apples

green apple and pea shoot salad, beef carpaccio with salsa verde and, 48–50, **49**

green apple salad, Fontina Val d'Aosta with chestnut honey and, 253

grilled blood sausage with green apples and saba, 38–39

Apricot jam, pecorino Toscano with, 245

Artichokes, 70

angel hair frittata with artichokes and black pepper pecorino, 192–93

baby artichokes with lemon-garlic bread crumbs, 70–72

Arugula

Scamorza with arugula and oranges, **246**, 247

Asiago cheese, 244

with glazed cipolline onions, **254**, 255

with shaved fennel salad (substitute), 244

Asparagus

bruschetta with shaved white and green asparagus and pecorino Toscano, 113

crostini with chopped egg and asparagus, 138–40, **139**

Assaggio, 11–39

about, 11

baby beets with flat-leaf parsley and mint vinaigrette, 27–28, **29**

fava and yellow beans with radicchio, goat cheese, and anise-orange vinaigrette, 12–13

four-olive mix, 30

giardiniera, 32–33

grilled blood sausage with green apples and saba, 38–39

grilled shrimp wrapped in pancetta with lemon aioli, 34–35

marinated white anchovy and dandelion salad, **16**, 17–18

roasted cipolline with aged balsamic and garlic bread crumbs, 14–15

roasted Medjool dates with Gorgonzola, bacon, and toasted walnuts, 36–37, **37**

sautéed drunken wild mushrooms, 31

Tramonto's razor clams casino, 19–22, **21**

zucchini blossoms stuffed with smoked mozzarella and ricotta, 23–26, **25**

Aunt Dorothy's tripe with spicy tomato sauce, 102–3

Australian Murray River salt, 67

Avocado carpaccio with pears and ricotta salata, 90–91

b

Baby octopus, 199

grilled baby octopus and

fingerling potato salad, 197–200, **198**

Baccala, crostini with, 154–55

Bacon

roasted Medjool dates with Gorgonzola, bacon, and toasted walnuts, 36–37, **37**

truffled scrambled egg and bacon panini, 170–72, **171**

Balsamic vinegar, 9

crostini with chicken livers and balsamic, 152–53

multicolor heirloom tomatoes with burrata and aged balsamic, **82**, 83

roasted cipolline with aged balsamic and garlic bread crumbs, 14–15

Bartolotta, Paul, 79

Basil

basil oil, 101; Grana Padano flan with, 100–101

basil pesto, 26; zucchini blossoms stuffed with smoked mozzarella and ricotta with, 23–24, **25**

Batali, Mario, 126

Beans

bruschetta with borlotti beans and prosciutto di Parma, 121–23, **122**

cannellini, homemade, 93; sautéed escarole and cannellini beans, 92–93

farro with vegetables, 194–96, **195**

fava and yellow beans with radicchio, goat cheese, and anise-orange vinaigrette, 12–13

green and yellow beans with sherry vinaigrette, 206

in marinated white anchovy and dandelion salad, 17–18

white beans with stewed tomatoes, 228–30, **229**

See also Ceci beans

Beccofino, 51

Beef

beef carpaccio, 41; with green

apple and pea shoot salad and salsa verde, 48–50, **49**

bruschetta with skirt steak and tapenade, 129–31, **130**

crostini with beef tartare and white truffle oil, 143–44

meat ragu, creamy soft polenta with, 231–33, **232**

stuffed rice balls, 238–39

See also Bresaola

Beets

  baby beets with flat-leaf parsley and mint vinaigrette, 27–28, **29**

Bella Luna, 34

Bell peppers. *See* Peppers

Bianco, Chris, 31

Blood orange(s)

  sea bass carpaccio with blood orange, capers, and green olives, 64, **65**

  speck with blood oranges and almond mustard, 96–97

Blood sausage, grilled, with green apples and saba, 38–39

Bocconcini, 69–109

  about, 69

  Aunt Dorothy's tripe with spicy tomato sauce, 102–3

  baby artichokes with lemon-garlic bread crumbs, 70–72

  braised fennel with orange, 74, 75

  bresaola with egg yolk and Parmesan, 104

  broccoli rabe with slivered garlic, 73

  ceci bean, shaved celery, and cabbage salad, 105–6

  eggplant Calabrese, 87–88

  fonduta, 79

  Grana Padano flan with basil olive oil, 100–101

  grilled porcini mushrooms with crumbled Sottobosco cheese, 98–99

  grilled radicchio di Treviso with garlic vinaigrette, 76–78, 77

  jumbo crawfish with diavolo vinaigrette, 84, 85–86

  mini veal meatballs with caramelized onions, 107–9, **108**

multicolor heirloom tomatoes with burrata and aged balsamic, **82**, 83

prosciutto di Parma with three melons, 89

salted fingerling potatoes and truffle butter, 94–95

salumi with peaches and watercress, 80, **81**

sautéed escarole and cannellini beans, 92–93

speck with blood oranges and almond mustard, 96–97

Borlotti beans, bruschetta with prosciutto di Parma and, 121–23, **122**

Bottarga, 51, 52

  tartare of halibut, pickled red onion, and shaved bottarga, 51–53

Bread

  pappa pomodoro, 218, **219**

  Tuscan panzanella, 207–9, **208**

  See also Bruschetta; Cicchetti; Crostini; Panini

Bread crumbs

  garlic bread crumbs, 15; roasted cipolline with aged balsamic and, 14–15

  lemon-garlic bread crumbs, 71–72; baby artichokes with, 70–71; cauliflower with golden raisins and lemon-garlic bread crumbs, 236, **237**

Bresaola with egg yolk and Parmesan, 104

Broccoli rabe with slivered garlic, 73

Bruschetta, 111–31

  about, 111

  basic, Rick's, 112

  with borlotti beans and prosciutto di Parma, 121–23, **122**

  with eggplant caponata, 124–25

  with fennel and green olives, 114–15

  with lardo and extra virgin olive oil, 126

  with roasted minted zucchini and

Fontina Val d'Aosta, 118–20, **119**

  with roasted peppers and white anchovies, 116–17

  with shaved white and green asparagus and pecorino Toscano, 113

  with skirt steak and tapenade, 129–31, **130**

  with spicy ceci bean puree, 127–28

Burrata cheese, 83

  multicolor heirloom tomatoes with burrata and aged balsamic, **82**, 83

Butter, 133, 135

  lemon butter, smoked salmon and green tomato cicchetti with, 180

  truffle butter, salted fingerling potatoes and, 94–95

  truffle butter cicchetti, 185

C

Cabbage

  braised red cabbage with pancetta, 235

  ceci bean, shaved celery, and cabbage salad, 105–6

Caciocavallo cheese, 87

Cannellini beans

  homemade, 93

  sautéed escarole and cannellini beans, 92–93

  white beans with stewed tomatoes, 228–30, **229**

Cantinetta Antinori, 64

Capers

  caper aioli, fried smelts with, 203–5, **204**

  sea bass carpaccio with blood orange, capers, and green olives, 64, **65**

Caponata

  bruschetta with eggplant caponata, 124–25

Caramelized onions

  crostini with prosciutto di Parma and caramelized onions, 146

fried eggplant, caramelized onion, and provolone panini, 164–67, **165**
mini veal meatballs with caramelized onions, 107–9, **108**
Cardoons al forno, 226–27
Carpaccio
  avocado carpaccio with pears and ricotta salata, 90–91
  beef carpaccio, 41; with green apple and pea shoot salad and salsa verde, 48–50, **49**
  hamachi carpaccio with piquillo peppers and grilled lemon, 42–44, **43**
  sea bass carpaccio with blood orange, capers, and green olives, 64, **65**
Carrots
  giardiniera, 32–33
Cauliflower
  cauliflower with golden raisins and lemon-garlic bread crumbs, 236, **237**
  giardiniera, 32–33
Ceci beans
  bruschetta with spicy ceci bean puree, 127–28
  ceci bean, shaved celery, and cabbage salad, 105–6
  homemade ceci beans, 106
Celery
  ceci bean, shaved celery, and cabbage salad, 105–6
  giardiniera, 32–33
  speck with blood oranges and almond mustard, 96–97
Champagne vinaigrette, ceci bean, shaved celery, and cabbage salad with, 105–6
Cheese, 241–56
  about, 241, 256
  Asiago cheese with glazed cipolline onions, **254**, 255
  fonduta, 79
  Fontina, Gouda, and tomato panini, 158
  Fontina Val d'Aosta with green apple salad and chestnut honey, 253

format di ricotta with vanilla-poached persimmon, 242–43
goat cheese with frisée salad and extra virgin olive oil, 256
Gorgonzola dolce with roasted pears and spiced walnuts, **250**, 251–52
pecorino Toscano with apricot jam, 245
Scamorza with arugula and oranges, **246**, 247
stuffed rice balls, 238–39
Taleggio with quince paste and Marcona almonds, 248–49
three-cheese panini, 159
Umbriaco al Vino Rosa cheese with shaved fennel salad, 244
See also specific types
Chez Panisse, 184
Chicken
  grilled chicken with soppressata salumi and black olive aioli panini, 173–74
Chicken livers
  crostini with chicken livers and balsamic, 152–53
Chickpeas
  bruschetta with spicy ceci bean puree, 127–28
  ceci bean, shaved celery, and cabbage salad, 105–6
  homemade ceci beans, 106
Cibreo, 104
Cicchetti, 179–89
  about, 179
  coppa and pecorino Toscano, 189
  creamy foie gras, 181
  fresh ricotta and sun-dried tomato, 188
  Gorgonzola with pear, 186, **187**
  shrimp salad, **182**, 183
  smoked salmon and green tomato with lemon butter, 180
  truffle, 185
  tuna conserva, 184
Cinnamon cranberries, parsnips with, 234
Cipolline onions
  Asiago cheese with glazed cipolline onions, **254**, 255

roasted cipolline onions with aged balsamic and garlic bread crumbs, 14–15
Citrus-marinated sea scallops, 63
Clams, 19
  crostini with chopped clams and pancetta, 141–42
  Tramonto's razor clams casino, 19–22, **21**
Coppa and pecorino Toscano cicchetti, 189
Corn
  farro with vegetables, 194–96, **195**
Crab
  crostini with lump crab salad and extra virgin olive oil, 136, **137**
Cranberries
  parsnips with cinnamon cranberries, 234
Crawfish
  jumbo crawfish with diavolo vinaigrette, **84**, 85–86
Crostini, 133–55
  about, 133
  basic, Rick's, 134
  with beef tartare and white truffle oil, 143–44
  with chicken livers and balsamic, 152–53
  with chopped clams and pancetta, 141–42
  with chopped egg and asparagus, 138–40, **139**
  crostini baccala, 154–55
  with grilled Black Mission figs and orange mascarpone, 149–51, **150**
  with lump crab salad and extra virgin olive oil, 136, **137**
  with prosciutto di Parma and caramelized onions, 146
  with spicy Italian sausage and spinach, 145
  with wild mushroom ragu, 147–48
Crudo, 41–65
  about, 41
  beef carpaccio with green apple

and pea shoot salad and salsa
verde, 48–50, **49**

citrus-marinated sea scallops,
63

crusted ahi tuna with
pomegranate vinaigrette,
60–62, **61**

cured salmon with shaved fennel
and radish salad, 45–47

fluke with cucumber, lime salt,
and Moscato grapes, 58–59

hamachi carpaccio with piquillo
peppers and grilled lemon,
42–44, **43**

marinated swordfish with mint
and preserved Meyer lemon,
56–57

oysters with red wine vinaigrette,
54–55

sea bass carpaccio with blood
orange, capers, and green
olives, 64, **65**

tartare of halibut, pickled red
onion, and shaved bottarga,
51–53

Crusted ahi tuna with pomegranate
vinaigrette, 60–62, **61**

Cucumbers
fluke with cucumber, lime salt,
and Moscato grapes, 58–59
pickled red onion and cucumber,
52–53; tartare of halibut and
shaved bottarga with, 51

Cured salmon with shaved fennel
and radish salad, 45–47

Cyprus black salt, 67

d

Dandelion greens
marinated white anchovy and
dandelion salad, 17–18

Dates
roasted Medjool dates with
Gorgonzola, bacon, and toasted
walnuts, 36–37, **37**

Diavolo vinaigrette, jumbo crawfish
with, **84**, 85–86

DiGregorio, David, 107

e

Egg(s)
angel hair frittata with artichokes
and black pepper pecorino,
192–93

bresaola with egg yolk and
Parmesan, 104

crostini with chopped egg and
asparagus, 138–40, **139**

frittata with prosciutto, potato,
and spinach, 201–2

truffled scrambled egg and bacon
panini, 170–72, **171**

Eggplant
bruschetta with eggplant
caponata, 124–25
eggplant Calabrese, 87–88
fried eggplant, caramelized onion,
and provolone panini, 164–67,
165
giardiniera, 32–33

Equipment sources, 260–61

Escarole
sautéed escarole and cannellini
beans, 92–93

f

Farro with vegetables, 194–96, **195**

Fava beans
fava and yellow beans with
radicchio, goat cheese, and
anise-orange vinaigrette, 12–13

Fennel
braised fennel with orange, **74**, 75
bruschetta with fennel and green
olives, 114–15
farro with vegetables, 194–96,
195
shaved fennel and radish salad,
cured salmon with, 45–47
speck with blood oranges and
almond mustard, 96–97
Tuscan panzanella, 207–9, **208**
Umbriaco al Vino Rosa cheese
with shaved fennel salad, 244

Figs
crostini with grilled Black

Mission figs and orange
mascarpone, 149–51, **150**

Fish
Abruzzi swordfish roll-ups,
215–17, **216**
crostini baccala, 154–55
crusted ahi tuna with
pomegranate vinaigrette,
60–62, **61**
cured salmon with shaved fennel
and radish salad, 45–47
fluke with cucumber, lime salt,
and Moscato grapes, 58–59
fried smelts with caper aioli,
203–5, **204**
hamachi carpaccio with piquillo
peppers and grilled lemon,
42–44, **43**
marinated swordfish with mint
and preserved Meyer lemon,
56–57
sea bass carpaccio with blood
orange, capers, and green
olives, 64, **65**
smoked salmon and green tomato
with lemon butter cichetti,
180
tartare of halibut, pickled red
onion, and shaved bottarga,
51–53
tuna conserva cichetti, 184
Venetian-style stuffed sardines,
224–25

Flan, Grana Padano, with basil
olive oil, 100–101

Fleur de sel, 67

Fluke with cucumber, lime salt, and
Moscato grapes, 58–59

Foie gras, 181
creamy foie gras cichetti, 181

Folse, John, 54

Fonduta, 79

Fontina cheese, 79, 120, 253
bruschetta with roasted minted
zucchini and Fontina Val
d'Aosta, 118–20, **119**
fonduta, 79
Fontina, Gouda, and tomato
panini, 158
Fontina Val d'Aosta with green

apple salad and chestnut honey, 253

three-cheese panini, 159

Format di ricotta with vanilla-poached persimmon, 242–43

Four-olive mix, 30

Frisée salad, goat cheese with extra virgin olive oil and, 256

Frittata

angel hair frittata with artichokes and black pepper pecorino, 192–93

frittata with prosciutto, potato, and spinach, 201–2

g

Gand, Gale, 114

Garlic

broccoli rabe with slivered garlic, 73

garlic bread crumbs, 15; roasted cipolline with aged balsamic and, 14–15

lemon-garlic bread crumbs, 71–72; baby artichokes with, 70–71

lobster with garlic and Parmigiano-Reggiano, 213–14

roasted garlic aioli, 161; PLT (pancetta, lettuce, and tomato panini) with, 160–61

steamed black mussels with garlic and spicy pepperoni, 223

vinaigrette, grilled radicchio di Treviso with, 76–78, 77

Gentile, Adeline, 12

Gentile, Vincenzo, 189

Giardiniera, 32–33

Goat cheese

fava and yellow beans with radicchio, goat cheese, and anise-orange vinaigrette, 12–13

goat cheese spread, 169; grilled portobello mushrooms with herb goat cheese panini, 168–69

goat cheese with frisée salad and extra virgin olive oil, 256

Gomiero, Lucio, 78

Gorgonzola

Gorgonzola dolce with roasted pears and spiced walnuts, 250, 251–52

Gorgonzola with pear cicchetti, 186, 187

roasted Medjool dates with Gorgonzola, bacon, and toasted walnuts, 36–37, 37

Gouda cheese

Fontina, Gouda, and tomato panini, 158

Grana Padano flan with basil olive oil, 100–101

Grapes

fluke with cucumber, lime salt, and Moscato grapes, 58–59

Green beans

farro with vegetables, 194–96, 195

green and yellow beans with sherry vinaigrette, 206

in marinated white anchovy and dandelion salad, 17–18

Green tomato

smoked salmon and green tomato with lemon butter cicchetti, 180

h

Halibut

tartare of halibut, pickled red onion, and shaved bottarga, 51–53

Ham

Robiola and honey-baked ham with mustard mayonnaise panini, 175–77, 176

See also Prosciutto; Speck

Hamachi carpaccio with piquillo peppers and grilled lemon, 42–44, 43

Hawaiian red salt, 67

Herbs

goat cheese spread, 169; grilled portobello mushrooms with herb goat cheese panini, 168–69

herb oil, 200

salsa verde, 50

soft herb vinaigrette, 18; marinated white anchovy and dandelion salad with, 16, 17–18

Honey

Fontina Val d'Aosta with green apple salad and chestnut honey, 253

roasted cipolline with aged balsamic and garlic bread crumbs, 14–15

i

Il Cantinori, 145

Il Latini, 89

Ingredients sources, 257–60, 261

Italian sausage with roasted peppers and onions, 220–22, 221

j

Jam, apricot, pecorino Toscano with, 245

k

Kosher salt, 67

l

Lardo, bruschetta with extra virgin olive oil and, 126

Le Bernardin, 154

Lemon

citrus-marinated sea scallops, 63

grilled lemon, hamachi carpaccio with piquillo peppers and, 42–44, 43

lemon aioli, grilled shrimp wrapped in pancetta with, 34–35

lemon-garlic bread crumbs, 71–72; baby artichokes with,

70–71; cauliflower with golden raisins and lemon-garlic bread crumbs, 236, **237**

lemon sauce, Abruzzi swordfish roll-ups with, 215–17, **216**

lemon vinaigrette, 47, 200; cured salmon with shaved fennel and radish salad with, 45–46

preserved Meyer lemon, 57; marinated swordfish with mint and, 56

smoked salmon and green tomato with lemon butter cicchetti, 180

Lime salt, 59

fluke with cucumber, Moscato grapes, and, 58

Lobster

lobsters with diavolo vinaigrette, 85–86

lobster with garlic and Parmigiano-Reggiano, 213–14

Lump crab salad, crostini with extra virgin olive oil and, 136, **137**

m

Mail-order sources, 257–61

Maldon salt, 67

lime salt, 59

Marcona almonds

roasted spaghetti squash with vanilla and Marcona almonds, 210–12, **211**

Taleggio with quince paste and Marcona almonds, 248–49

Marinated swordfish with mint and preserved Meyer lemon, 56–57

Marinated vegetables (giardiniera), 32–33

Marinated white anchovy and dandelion salad, **16**, 17–18

Mascarpone cheese

crostini with grilled Black Mission figs and orange mascarpone, 149–51, **150**

Mayonnaise

black olive aioli, 174; grilled

chicken with soppressata salumi and black olive aioli panini, 173–74

caper aioli, fried smelts with, 203–5, **204**

lemon aioli, grilled shrimp wrapped in pancetta with, 34–35

mustard mayonnaise, 177; Robiola and honey-baked ham with mustard mayonnaise panini, 175–77, **176**

roasted garlic aioli, 161; PLT (pancetta, lettuce, and tomato panini) with, 160–61

tarragon mayonnaise, 140; crostini with chopped egg and asparagus with, 138, **139**

Meat(s)

Aunt Dorothy's tripe with spicy tomato sauce, 102–3

beef carpaccio, 41; with green apple and pea shoot salad and salsa verde, 48–50, **49**

bresaola with egg yolk and Parmesan, 104

bruschetta with skirt steak and tapenade, 129–31, **130**

creamy foie gras cichetti, 181

creamy soft polenta with meat ragu, 231–33, **232**

crostini with beef tartare and white truffle oil, 143–44

crostini with spicy Italian sausage and spinach, 145

grilled blood sausage with green apples and saba, 38–39

Italian sausage with roasted peppers and onions, 220–22, **221**

mini veal meatballs with caramelized onions, 107–9, **108**

salumi with peaches and watercress, 80, **81**

speck with blood oranges and almond mustard, 96–97

stuffed rice balls, 238–39

See also Chicken; Pancetta; Prosciutto

Melon

prosciutto di Parma with three melons, 89

Meyer lemon, preserved, 57

marinated swordfish with mint and, 56

Mini veal meatballs with caramelized onions, 107–9, **108**

Mint

bruschetta with roasted minted zucchini and Fontina Val d'Aosta, 118–20, **119**

marinated swordfish with preserved Meyer lemon and mint, 56–57

mint vinaigrette, 28; baby beets with flat-leaf parsley and, 27–28, **29**

Moscato grapes, fluke with cucumber, lime salt, and, 58–59

Mozzarella cheese

fresh mozzarella, roasted red peppers, and pistachio pesto panini, 162–63

stuffed rice balls, 238–39

three-cheese panini, 159

zucchini blossoms stuffed with smoked mozzarella and ricotta, 23–26, **25**

Murray River salt, 67

Mushrooms

crostini with wild mushroom ragu, 147–48

giardiniera, 32–33

grilled porcini mushrooms with crumbled Sottobosco cheese, 98–99

grilled portobello mushrooms with herb goat cheese panini, 168–69

porcini cicchetti (substitute), 185

sautéed drunken wild mushrooms, 31

Mussels

steamed black mussels with garlic and spicy pepperoni, 223

Mustard

mustard mayonnaise, 177; Robiola and honey-baked ham

with mustard mayonnaise panini, 175–77, **176**
speck with blood oranges and almond mustard, 96–97

O

Octopus
grilled baby octopus and fingerling potato salad, 197–200, **198**
Olive oil, 9, 78
basil oil, 101; Grana Padano flan with basil olive oil, 100–101
bruschetta with lardo and extra virgin olive oil, 126
herb oil, 200
Olives
black olive aioli, 174; grilled chicken with soppressata salumi and black olive aioli panini, 173–74
bruschetta with fennel and green olives, 114–15
four-olive mix, 30
sea bass carpaccio with blood orange, capers, and green olives, 64, **65**
Tramonto's tapenade, 131; bruschetta with skirt steak and tapenade, 129–31, **130**
Onions
Asiago cheese with glazed cipolline onions, 254, 255
crostini with prosciutto di Parma and caramelized onions, 146
fried eggplant, caramelized onion, and provolone panini, 164–67, **165**
Italian sausage with roasted peppers and onions, 220–22, **221**
mini veal meatballs with caramelized onions, 107–9, **108**
pickled red onion and cucumber, 52–53; tartare of halibut and shaved bottarga with, 51–52
roasted cipolline with aged

balsamic and garlic bread crumbs, 14–15
Orange(s)
anise-orange vinaigrette, 13; fava and yellow beans with radicchio, goat cheese, and, 12
braised fennel with orange, 74, 75
citrus-marinated sea scallops, 63
crostini with grilled Black Mission figs and orange mascarpone, 149–51, **150**
Scamorza with arugula and oranges, **246**, 247
sea bass carpaccio with blood orange, capers, and green olives, 64, **65**
speck with blood oranges and almond mustard, 96–97
Osteria Via Stato, 107
Oysters with red wine vinaigrette, 54–55

P

Pancetta
braised red cabbage with pancetta, 235
crostini with chopped clams and pancetta, 141–42
grilled shrimp wrapped in pancetta with lemon aioli, 34–35
PLT (pancetta, lettuce, and tomato panini), 160–61
Pandel, Chris, 234
Panini, 157–77
about, 157
Fontina, Gouda, and tomato, 158
fresh mozzarella, roasted red peppers, and pistachio pesto, 162–63
fried eggplant, caramelized onion, and provolone, 164–67, **165**
grilled chicken with soppressata salumi and black olive aioli, 173–74
grilled portobello mushrooms with herb goat cheese, 168–69

PLT (pancetta, lettuce, and tomato), 160–61
Robiola and honey-baked ham with mustard mayonnaise, 175–77, **176**
three-cheese panini, 159
truffled scrambled egg and bacon, 170–72, **171**
Panzanella, Tuscan, 207–9, **208**
Pappa pomodoro, 218, **219**
Parmesan cheese
bresaola with egg yolk and Parmesan, 104
lobster with garlic and Parmigiano-Reggiano, 213–14
Parsley
baby beets with flat-leaf parsley and mint vinaigrette, 27–28, **29**
herb oil, 200
salsa verde, 50
Parsnips with cinnamon cranberries, 234
Pasta
angel hair frittata with artichokes and black pepper pecorino, 192–93
Peaches
peach jam, pecorino Toscano with (substitute), 245
salumi with watercress and peaches, 80, **81**
Pears
avocado carpaccio with pears and ricotta salata, 90–91
Gorgonzola dolce with roasted pears and spiced walnuts, **250**, 251–52
Gorgonzola with pear cicchetti, 186, **187**
Pea shoots
green apple and pea shoot salad, beef carpaccio with salsa verde and, 48–50, **49**
Peck, 206
Pecorino cheese, 113, 245
angel hair frittata with artichokes and black pepper pecorino, 192–93
bruschetta with shaved white and

green asparagus and pecorino
Toscano, 113
coppa and pecorino Toscano
cicchetti, 189
pecorino Toscano with apricot
jam, 245
Pepperoni
steamed black mussels with garlic
and spicy pepperoni, 223
Peppers
bruschetta with roasted peppers
and white anchovies, 116–17
fresh mozzarella, roasted red
peppers, and pistachio pesto
panini, 162–63
giardiniera, 32–33
hamachi carpaccio with piquillo
peppers and grilled lemon,
42–44, **43**
Italian sausage with roasted
peppers and onions, 220–22,
221
piquillo, in jumbo crawfish with
diavolo vinaigrette, 85–86
roasting, 117
Tuscan panzanella, 207–9, **208**
Persimmons
format di ricotta with vanilla-
poached persimmon, 242–43
Pesto
basil pesto, 26; zucchini blossoms
stuffed with smoked
mozzarella and ricotta with,
23–24, **25**
pistachio pesto, 163; fresh
mozzarella, roasted red
peppers, and pistachio pesto
panini, 162
Picchi, Fabio, 104
Pickled red onion and cucumber,
52–53
tartare of halibut and shaved
bottarga with, 51–52
Pickled vegetables (giardiniera),
32–33
Pink Peruvian mountain salt, 67
Piquillo peppers, 44
hamachi carpaccio with piquillo
peppers and grilled lemon,
42–44, **43**

jumbo crawfish with diavolo
vinaigrette, **84**, 85–86
Pistachio pesto, 163
fresh mozzarella, roasted red
peppers, and pistachio pesto
panini, 162
Pizzeria Bianco, 31
Pizzeria Mozza, 168
PLT (pancetta, lettuce, and tomato
panini), 160–61
Plum jam, pecorino Toscano with
(subsitute), 245
Polenta
creamy soft polenta with meat
ragu, 231–33, **232**
Pomegranate vinaigrette, crusted ahi
tuna with, 60–62, **61**
Porcini mushrooms
grilled porcini mushrooms with
crumbled Sottobosco cheese,
98–99
porcini cicchetti (substitute),
185
Pork
meat ragu, creamy soft polenta
with, 231–233, **232**
See also Bacon; Ham; Pancetta;
Prosciutto; Salumi; Sausage;
Speck
Portobello mushrooms
grilled portobello mushrooms
with herb goat cheese panini,
168–69
Potatoes
frittata with prosciutto, potato,
and spinach, 201–2
grilled baby octopus and
fingerling potato salad,
197–200, **198**
salted fingerling potatoes and
truffle butter, 94–95
Preserved Meyer lemon, 57
marinated swordfish with mint
and, 56
Prosciutto
bruschetta with borlotti beans
and prosciutto di Parma,
121–23, **122**
crostini with prosciutto di Parma
and caramelized onions, 146

frittata with prosciutto, potato,
and spinach, 201–2
prosciutto di Parma with three
melons, 89
Provolone cheese
fried eggplant, caramelized onion,
and provolone panini, 164–67,
165
stuffed rice balls, 238–39
three-cheese panini, 159

q
Quince paste, Taleggio with
Marcona almonds and, 248–49

r
Radicchio, 76
fava and yellow beans with
radicchio, goat cheese, and
anise-orange vinaigrette, 12–13
grilled radicchio di Treviso with
garlic vinaigrette, 76–78, 77
Radishes
shaved fennel and radish salad,
cured salmon with, 45–47
Ragu
creamy soft polenta with meat
ragu, 231–33, **232**
crostini with wild mushroom
ragu, 147–48
Raisins
Asiago cheese with glazed
cipolline onions, 254, 255
cauliflower with golden raisins
and lemon-garlic bread crumbs,
236, **237**
Razor clams casino, Tramonto's,
19–22, **21**
Red cabbage
braised red cabbage with
pancetta, 235
Red peppers. *See* Peppers
Red wine vinaigrette, oysters with,
54–55
Rice
stuffed rice balls, 238–39

Ricotta cheese
  format di ricotta with vanilla-
    poached persimmon, 242–43
  fresh ricotta and sun-dried tomato
    cicchetti, 188
  zucchini blossoms stuffed with
    smoked mozzarella and ricotta,
    23–26, **25**
Ricotta salata, avocado carpaccio
  with pears and, 90–91
Ripert, Eric, 154
River Café, 124
Robiola and honey-baked ham with
  mustard mayonnaise panini,
  175–77, **176**
Rock salt, Tramonto's razor clams
  casino on, 22

S
Saba vinegar, 39
  grilled blood sausage with green
    apples and saba, 38–39
Salads
  avocado carpaccio with pears and
    ricotta salata, 90–91
  baby beets with flat-leaf parsley
    and mint vinaigrette, 27–28, **29**
  ceci bean, shaved celery, and
    cabbage salad, 105–6
  fava and yellow beans with
    radicchio, goat cheese, and
    anise-orange vinaigrette, 12–13
  frisée salad, goat cheese with
    extra virgin olive oil and, 256
  green and yellow beans with
    sherry vinaigrette, 206
  green apple and pea shoot salad,
    beef carpaccio with salsa verde
    and, 48–50, **49**
  green apple salad, Fontina Val
    d'Aosta with chestnut honey
    and, 253
  grilled baby octopus and
    fingerling potato salad,
    197–200, **198**
  grilled porcini mushrooms with
    crumbled Sottobosco cheese,
    98–99

lump crab salad, crostini with
  extra virgin olive oil and, 136,
  137
marinated white anchovy and
  dandelion salad, **16**, 17–18
multicolor heirloom tomatoes
  with burrata and aged
  balsamic, **82**, 83
shaved fennel and radish salad,
  cured salmon with, 45–47
shaved fennel salad, Umbriaco al
  Vino Rosa cheese with, 244
shrimp salad cicchetti, **182**, 183
Tuscan panzanella, 207–9, **208**
Salmon
  cured salmon with shaved fennel
    and radish salad, 45–47
  smoked salmon and green tomato
    with lemon butter cicchetti, 180
Salsa verde, 50
  beef carpaccio with green apple
    and pea shoot salad and salsa
    verde, 48–50, **49**
Salt, 9, **66**, 67
  lime salt, 59; fluke with
    cucumber, Moscato grapes, and,
    58
  rock salt, Tramonto's razor clams
    casino on, 22
Salt cod
  crostini baccala, 154–55
Salted fingerling potatoes and truffle
  butter, 94–95
Salumi, 80, 173
  coppa and pecorino Toscano
    cichetti, 189
  grilled chicken with soppressata
    salumi and black olive aioli
    panini, 173–74
  salumi with peaches and
    watercress, 80, **81**
  See also Bresaola; Prosciutto;
    Sausage
Sandwiches. See Cicchetti; Panini
Sardines
  Venetian-style stuffed sardines,
    224–25
Sauces
  lemon sauce, Abruzzi swordfish
    roll-ups with, 215–17, **216**

salsa verde, 50
tomato sauce, 167; fried eggplant,
  caramelized onion, and
  provolone panini with,
  164–66, **165**; spicy, Aunt
  Dorothy's tripe with, 102–3
See also Mayonnaise; Ragu;
  Vinaigrette
Sausage
  crostini with spicy Italian sausage
    and spinach, 145
  grilled blood sausage with green
    apples and saba, 38–39
  Italian sausage with roasted
    peppers and onions, 220–22,
    221
  meat ragu, creamy soft polenta
    with, 231–33, **232**
  steamed black mussels with garlic
    and spicy pepperoni, 223
  See also Salumi
Sautéed escarole and cannellini
  beans, 92–93
Scallops
  citrus-marinated sea scallops, 63
Scamorza with arugula and oranges,
  246, 247
Seafood. See Fish; Shellfish; specific
  types
Sea scallops, citrus-marinated, 63
Shellfish
  citrus-marinated sea scallops, 63
  crostini with chopped clams and
    pancetta, 141–42
  crostini with lump crab salad and
    extra virgin olive oil, 136,
    137
  grilled shrimp wrapped in
    pancetta with lemon aioli,
    34–35
  jumbo crawfish with diavolo
    vinaigrette, **84**, 85–86
  lobster with garlic and
    Parmigiano-Reggiano,
    213–14
  oysters with red wine vinaigrette,
    54–55
  shrimp salad cicchetti, **182**, 183
  steamed black mussels with garlic
    and spicy pepperoni, 223

Tramonto's razor clams casino, 19–22, **21**

Sherry vinaigrette, green and yellow beans with, 206

Shrimp
grilled shrimp wrapped in pancetta with lemon aioli, 34–35
jumbo, with diavolo vinaigrette, 85–86
shrimp salad cicchetti, **182**, 183

Silverton, Nancy, 168

Simple syrup, 53

Skirt steak, bruschetta with tapenade and, 129–31, **130**

Smelts, fried, with caper aioli, 203–5, **204**

Smoked mozzarella
zucchini blossoms stuffed with smoked mozzarella and ricotta, 23–26, **25**

Smoked salmon and green tomato with lemon butter cicchetti, 180

Soft herb vinaigrette, 18
marinated white anchovy and dandelion salad with, **16**, 17–18

Soppressata
grilled chicken with soppressata salumi and black olive aioli panini, 173–74

Sottobosco cheese, 99
grilled porcini mushrooms with crumbled Sottobosco cheese, 98–99

Soups
pappa pomodoro, 218, **219**

Spaghetti squash, roasted, with vanilla and Marcona almonds, 210–12, **211**

Speck, 97
speck with blood oranges and almond mustard, 96–97

Spelt. *See* Farro

Spiced walnuts, 252
Gorgonzola dolce with roasted pears and, **250**, 251–52

Spicy ceci bean puree, bruschetta with, 127–28

Spicy Italian sausage, crostini with spinach and, 145

Spicy pepperoni, steamed black mussels with garlic and, 223

Spicy tomato sauce, Aunt Dorothy's tripe with, 102–3

Spinach
crostini with spicy Italian sausage and spinach, 145
frittata with prosciutto, potato, and spinach, 201–2

Squash
farro with vegetables, 194–96, **195**
roasted spaghetti squash with vanilla and Marcona almonds, 210–12, **211**
See also Zucchini

Stuffed rice balls, 238–39

Stuffed sardines, Venetian-style, 224–25

Sun-dried tomatoes
fresh ricotta and sun-dried tomato cicchetti, 188

Swordfish
Abruzzi swordfish roll-ups, 215–17, **216**
marinated swordfish with mint and preserved Meyer lemon, 56–57

Syrup, simple, 53

t

Taleggio with quince paste and Marcona almonds, 248–49

Tapenade, Tramonto's, 131
bruschetta with skirt steak and, 129–31, **130**

Tarragon mayonnaise, 140
crostini with chopped egg and asparagus with, 138, **139**

Tartare, beef, crostini with white truffle oil and, 143–44

Tartare of halibut, pickled red onion, and shaved bottarga, 51–53

Three-cheese panini, 159

Toasts. *See* Bruschetta; Crostini

Tomato(es)
farro with vegetables, 194–96, **195**
Fontina, Gouda, and tomato panini, 158
fresh ricotta and sun-dried tomato cicchetti, 188
multicolor heirloom tomatoes with burrata and aged balsamic, **82**, 83
pappa pomodoro, 218, **219**
PLT (pancetta, lettuce, and tomato panini), 160–61
smoked salmon and green tomato with lemon butter cicchetti, 180
spicy tomato sauce, Aunt Dorothy's tripe with, 102–3
stuffed rice balls, 238–39
tomato relish, zucchini blossoms stuffed with smoked mozzarella and ricotta with, 23–26, **25**
tomato sauce, 167; fried eggplant, caramelized onion, and provolone panini with, 164–66, **165**
Tuscan panzanella, 207–9, **208**
white beans with stewed tomatoes, 228–30, **229**

Trattoria Masuelli, 98

Trio, 75

Tripe
Aunt Dorothy's tripe with spicy tomato sauce, 102–3

Tru, 126

Truffles, truffle oil
crostini with beef tartare and white truffle oil, 143–44
fonduta with, 79
salted fingerling potatoes and truffle butter, 94–95
truffle cicchetti, 185
truffled scrambled egg and bacon panini, 170–72, **171**

Tuna
crusted ahi tuna with pomegranate vinaigrette, 60–62, **61**
tuna conserva cicchetti, 184

Tuscan panzanella, 207–9, **208**

u

Umbriaco al Vino Rosa cheese with shaved fennel salad, 244

v

Vanilla
    format di ricotta with vanilla-poached persimmon, 242–43
    roasted spaghetti squash with vanilla and Marcona almonds, 210–12, **211**
Veal
    mini veal meatballs with caramelized onions, 107–9, **108**
Vegetables
    farro with vegetables, 194–96, **195**
    pickled vegetables (giardiniera), 32–33
    See also specific vegetables
Venetian-style sandwiches. *See* Cichetti
Venetian-style stuffed sardines, 224–25
Vinaigrette
    anise-orange vinaigrette, 13; fava and yellow beans with radicchio, goat cheese, and, 12
    Champagne, ceci bean, shaved celery, and cabbage salad with, 105–6

diavolo, jumbo crawfish with, **84**, 85–86
    garlic, grilled radicchio di Treviso with, 76–78, *77*
    lemon vinaigrette, 47, 200; cured salmon with shaved fennel and radish salad with, 45–46
    mint vinaigrette, 28; baby beets with flat-leaf parsley and, 27–28, *29*
    pomegranate, crusted ahi tuna with, 60–62, *61*
    red wine, oysters with, 54–55
    sherry, green and yellow beans with, 206
    soft herb vinaigrette, 18; marinated white anchovy and dandelion salad with, **16**, 17–18

w

Walnuts
    Gorgonzola with pear cichetti with, 186, **187**
    roasted Medjool dates with Gorgonzola, bacon, and toasted walnuts, 36–37, *37*
    spiced walnuts, 252; Gorgonzola dolce with roasted pears and, **250**, 251–52
Watercress, salumi with peaches and, 80, **81**

White anchovies. *See* Anchovies
White beans
    white beans with stewed tomatoes, 228–30, **229**
    See also Cannellini beans
Wild mushrooms
    crostini with wild mushroom ragu, 147–48
    sautéed drunken wild mushrooms, 31

y

Yellow beans
    fava and yellow beans with radicchio, goat cheese, and anise-orange vinaigrette, 12–13

z

Zucchini
    bruschetta with roasted minted zucchini and Fontina Val d'Aosta, 118–20, **119**
    farro with vegetables, 194–96, **195**
Zucchini blossoms stuffed with smoked mozzarella and ricotta, 23–26, **25**